Legal information

© 2024
Author and Editor: M.Eng. Johannes Wild
A94689H39927F
Email: 3dtech@gmx.de

The complete imprint of the book can be found on the last pages!

This work is protected by copyright

Thank you so much for choosing this book!

Table of contents

Chapter 1 | Introduction

Thank you so much for choosing this book!

Attention: This book is the sequel to the book "CAD Projects with Tinkercad | 3D-Models Part 1" (ISBN: 9783987421129) as well as to the basics book "Tinkercad | Step by Step" (ISBN: 9783987420115). Anyone who has no previous knowledge of "Tinkercad" should work through these two books first. More information can be found on the last pages of this book. Therefore, the basics of "Tinkercad" will not be repeated in this book.

On the other hand, if you already have some experience in using "Tinkercad" or if you already have the mentioned books at home, then you can now look forward to creating more great projects. This way you can further deepen your skills in designing 3D models. As you may already know, I work as an engineer (M.Eng.), and in my books I try to teach you technical processes and the use of software in a simple and playful way.

In this book, we will get to know four more projects for designing 3D objects in "Tinkercad". Some of them are very complex, while others are a bit easier to create. But don't worry, we will work through these projects together and step by step. This will help you to use the different functions of "Tinkercad" even more confidently, and to learn one or the other new approach for the construction of your own 3D models. The more guided practice you have, the better you will be able to handle more complex projects of your own.

You probably already know that you can use "Tinkercad" not only to design 3D objects, but also to design electronic circuits and learn programming. However, this book – like the previous book – deals exclusively with the design of 3D models in "Tinkercad". You are welcome to have a look at the book "Arduino Projects with Tinkercad" (ISBN: 9783987420375) if you are also interested in electronics and programming. You can find more details on the last pages of this book.

And now let's get started! We'll start right away with the first project. In this one, we will try to build a table lamp!

Chapter 2 | 3D Model Project 1: Table Lamp

Our first project in this course will be the 3D model of a table lamp. This project is a good warm-up project because it is a bit less complex than the following ones. You can copy the CAD files to your own "Tinkercad" account using the following link.

https://tinyurl.com/3795bvjp

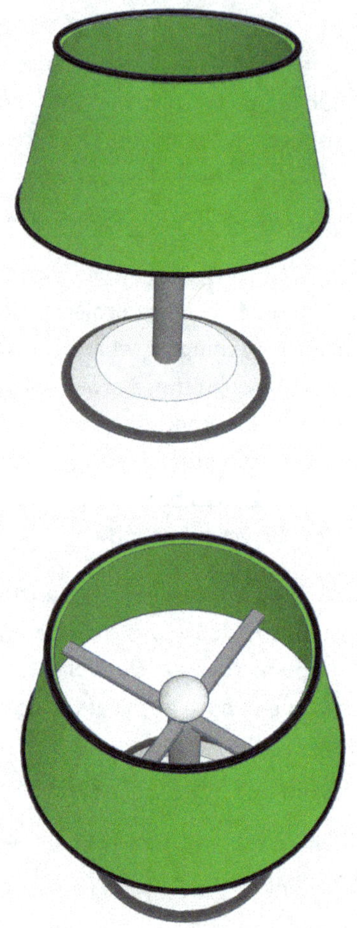

2.1 The lampshade

As the title of the chapter already indicates, we start the construction of the table lamp by building the green lampshade first. Before we do that, we create a new project for the 3D model in "Tinkercad". You can probably already do this yourself, but for this first project, I'll show you the steps one last time.

After logging into your own "Tinkercad" account (www.tinkercad.com) and being on the home page ①, to create a new project, click on the tab "Designs" ② in the area on the left, then click on the button "+ Create" ③ in the area on the right, and then select the option "3D Design" ④.

Now a new project opens, and we are ready to go. We will construct the lampshade from a basic body called "Cone". We can find it in the shape collection "Basic Shapes" ① in the middle section ②.

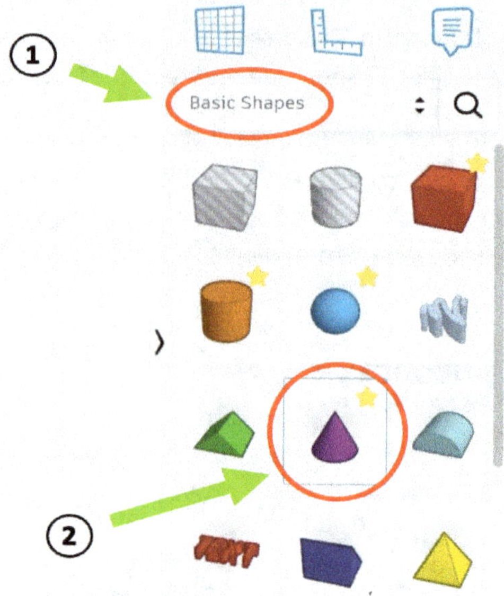

We place this body on the work plane using drag-and-drop and enlarge it in both directions to 50 mm each. To do this, click on the body, select a corner point ① and enter the dimensions ② and ③.

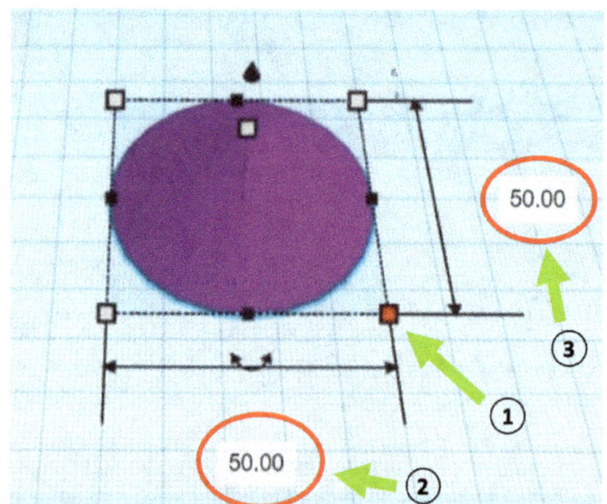

We also change the height of the cylindrical body to 28 mm. To do this, we click on the body, select the top boundary point ① and enter the dimension ②. In addition, we change the parameter "Top Radius" ③ to 7 mm and the value at "Sides" ④ to 64 so that the cone takes on the shape of the lampshade.

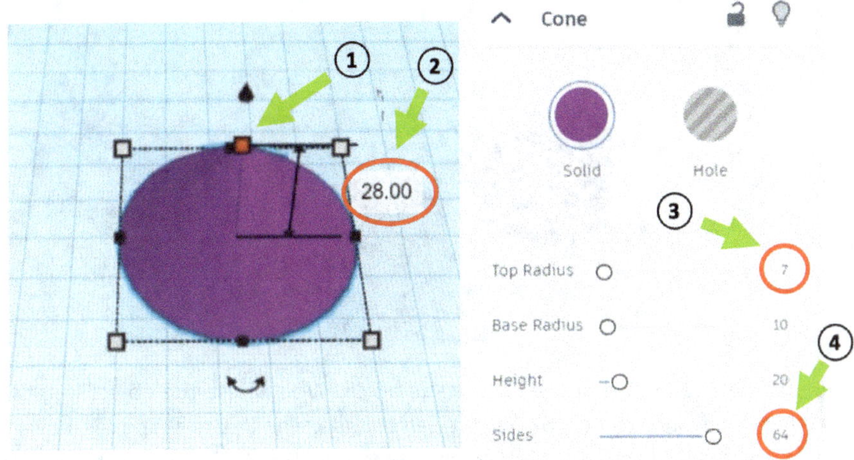

Since our lampshade is composed of two components, we duplicate the created body with the command "Duplicate and repeat" from the menu bar in the upper-left corner. To do this, click on the body ① and select the command ②. This places the duplicated part congruently on the original, so we move it slightly to the back left ③. We change the length and width of the duplicate to 48 mm each ④.

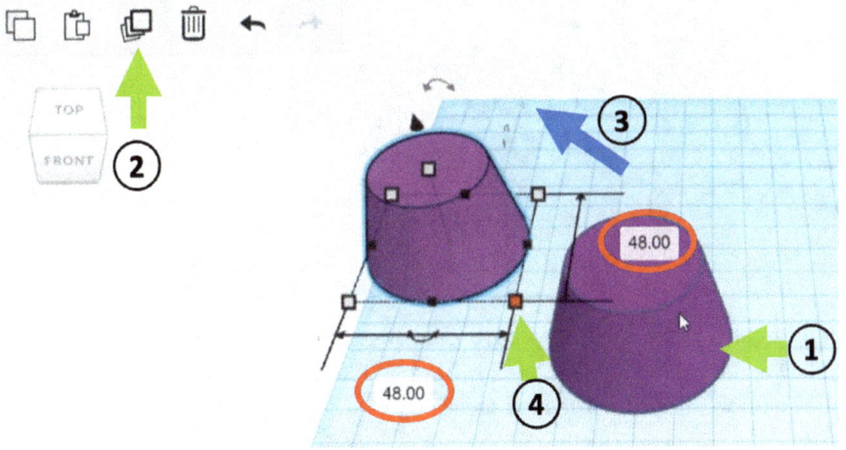

To do some preliminary work for the base of the table lamp, we double the initial shape again (① and ②) and move it to the back right, for example. This saves us having to recreate the object in a later step.

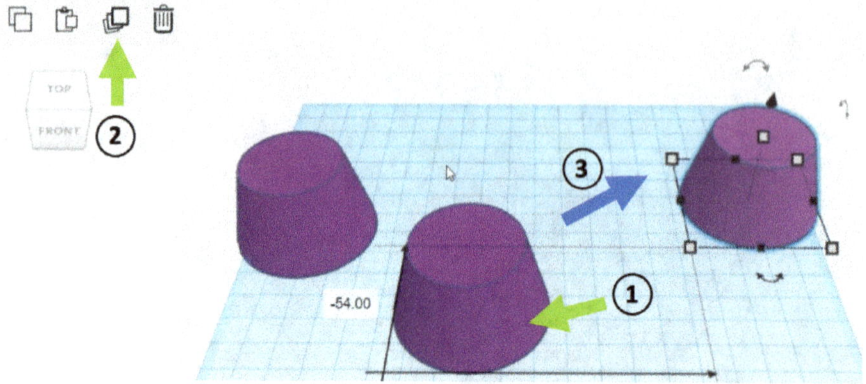

But now we'll take care of the lampshade again. We will use the object ①, that we created second, to hollow out the lampshade. For this to work, we have to switch from the selection "Solid" to the selection "Hole" ② in its settings. The object must be selected for this.

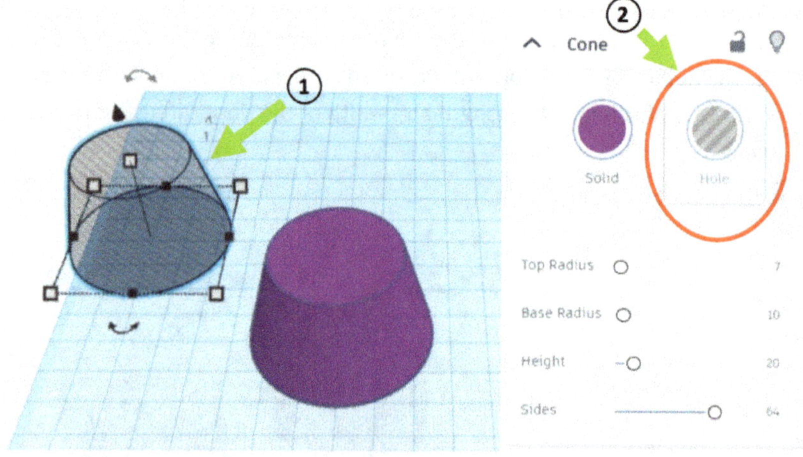

You can also think about how best to arrange the two objects so that we get the hollowed lampshade. If you already have an idea, you can try it out on your own. The solution follows on the next page.

------------------------------------- Solution follows here: -------------------------------------

For the alignment, we use the command "Align". For this, we select both objects with the mouse. For a multiple selection, we have to hold down the Shift key or span a rectangle.

Then we can select the command ① and – after the alignment points are displayed to us – click on the respective middle points ② and ③.

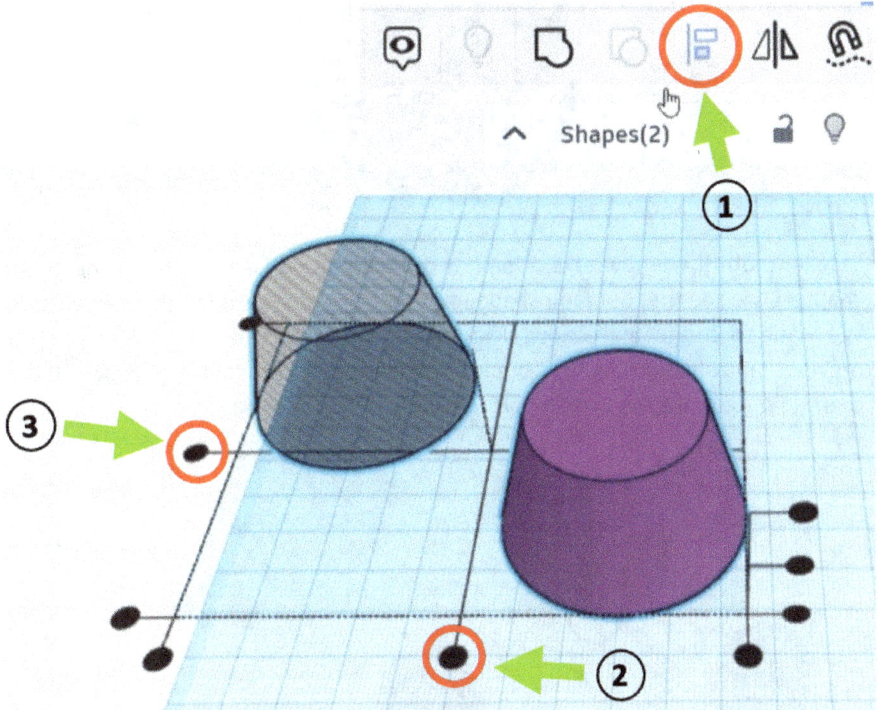

In order for the two objects to become one group, we then use the command "Group". Both objects must be selected for this.

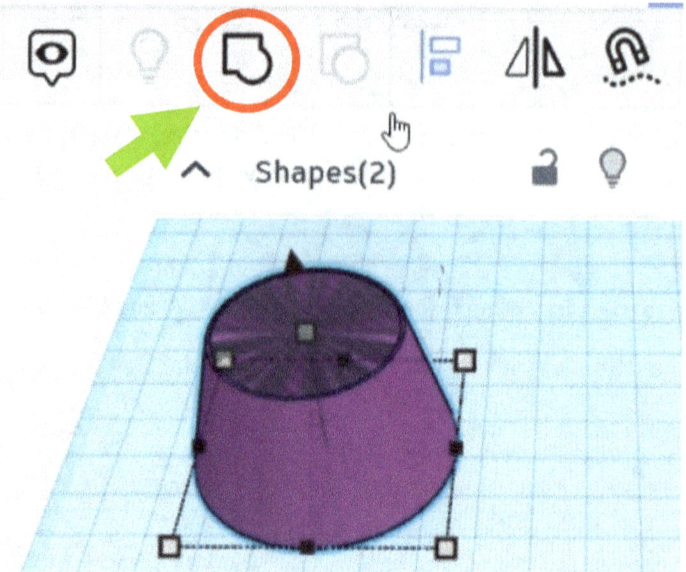

Excellent job! If we now take a look at the table lamp (see the beginning of the chapter), we see that our lampshade has additional bezels at the top and bottom. We want to create these now. The easiest way to do this is to duplicate the previous lampshade using the "Duplicate and repeat" command (① and ②) and then simply cut out the middle part using a box (③ and ④).

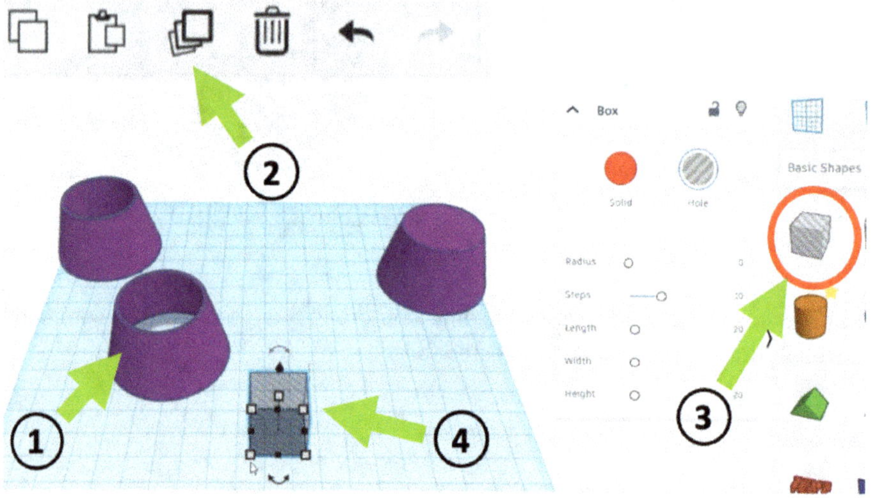

The box should be 79 mm long, 54.5 mm wide and 27 mm high (① - ③).

In addition, we want the cuboid to be centered in the lampshade, which we achieve by using the command "Align" ④ and selecting the alignment points ⑤-⑦. Finally, we group the two objects ⑧ so that the clipping is performed.

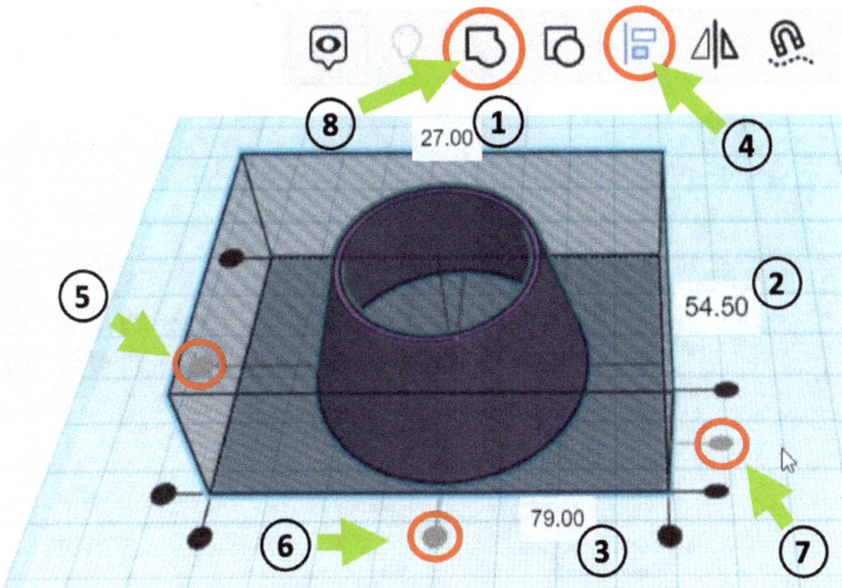

We thereby obtain this construct:

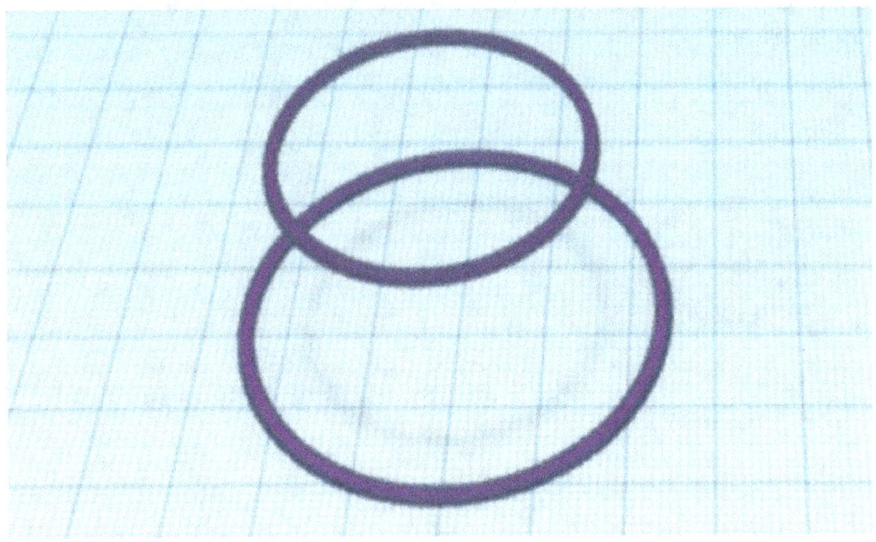

Before we connect the lampshade to the upper and lower bezels, we change its color. We can do this by clicking on the lampshade ① and selecting a color in the object's settings (② and ③).

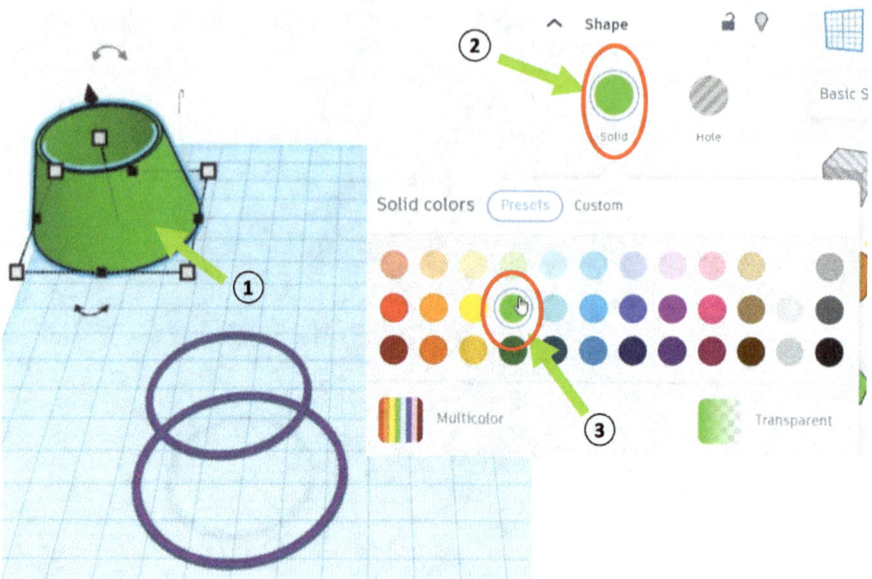

Furthermore, we change the color of the bezel – e.g. to black (① - ③) – and make another change to the dimensions, as the bezel needs to be a small bit larger than the lampshade.

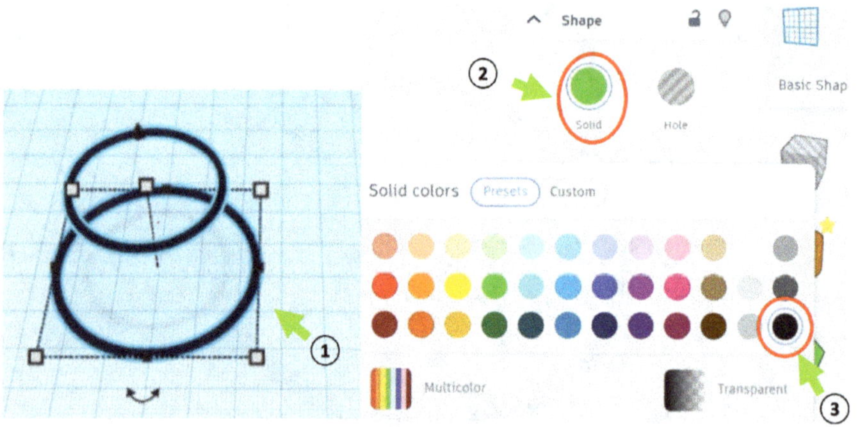

So, we change the length and width to 51 mm each and the height to 29 mm.

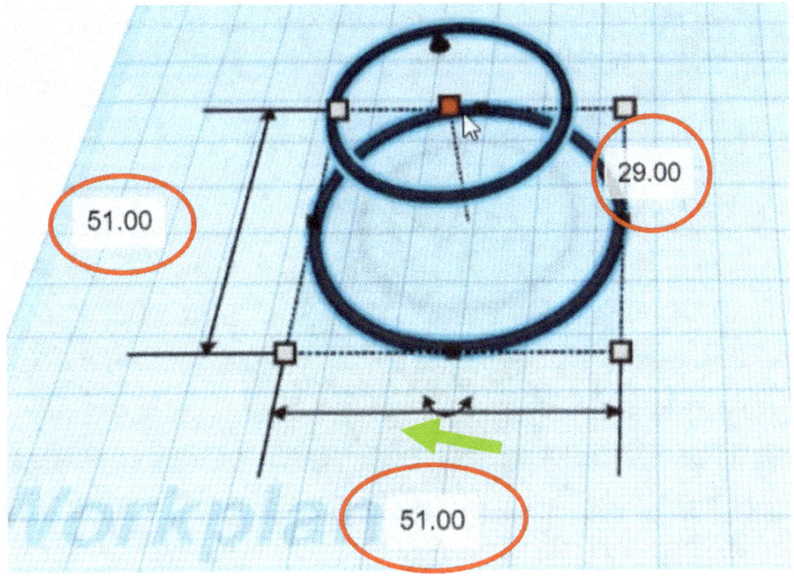

Now we can mark or select the two objects and then position them using the command "Align" ①. To do this, we click on the alignment points shown (② and ③).

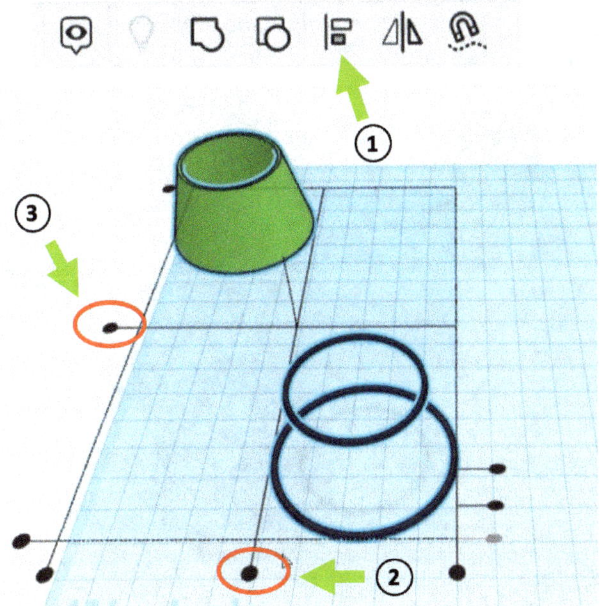

This will give us the finished lampshade. In the next chapter, we will take care of the base and the rest of the table lamp.

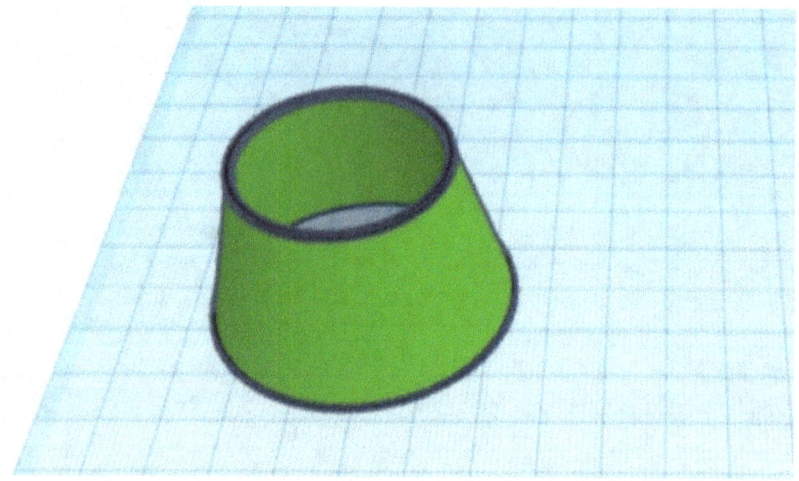

2.2 Base, rod and assembly of the table lamp

In the first part of this chapter, we would like to create the base for the table lamp. For this, we had already done some preliminary work in the previous chapter by duplicating the base body of the lampshade and moving it to the side. So, our starting point looks like this.

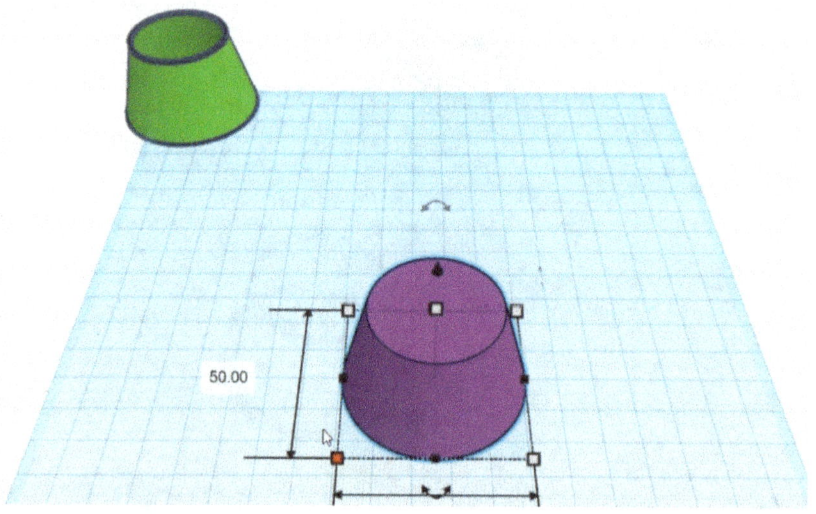

In the first step, we change the dimensions of the body to 38 mm each for the length and width and to 4 mm for the height ①. We also color the base white (② and ③).

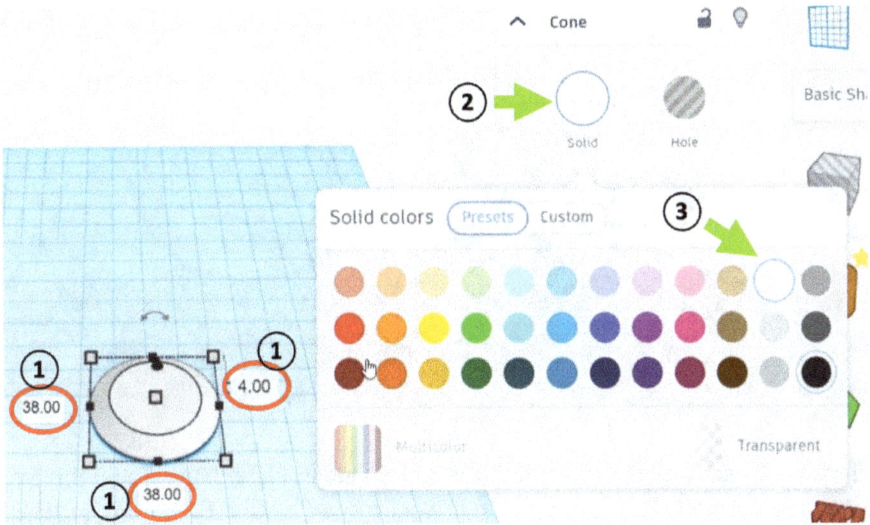

Similar to the lampshade, our base consists of two components. Therefore, we duplicate the body created so far using the command "Duplicate and repeat" (① and ②) and color it gray (③ and ④).

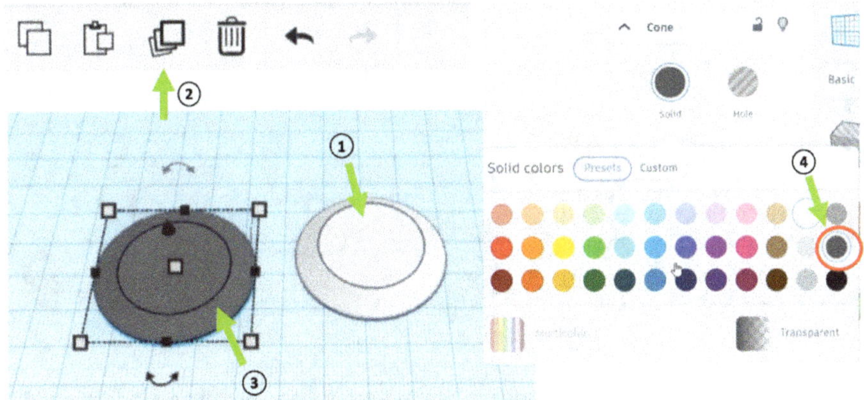

After that, we can unite the two bodies to the base of the lampshade. We do this as usual with the command "Align".

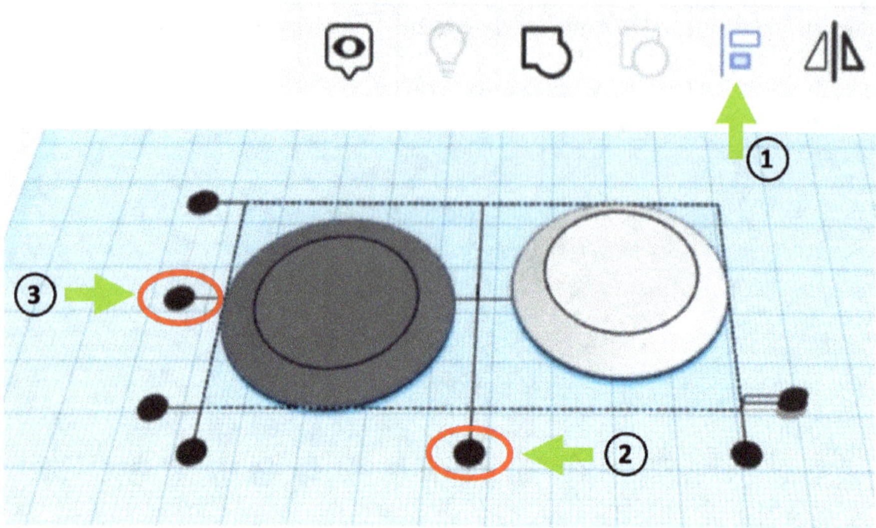

Next, we create the rod from which the lampshade will later hang. To do this, we will get a cylindrical base body on our work plane (① and ②). In its settings, increase the values for the settings "Sides", "Bevel" and "Bevel Segments" ③-⑤ to their respective maximum (64, 2.5, 10).

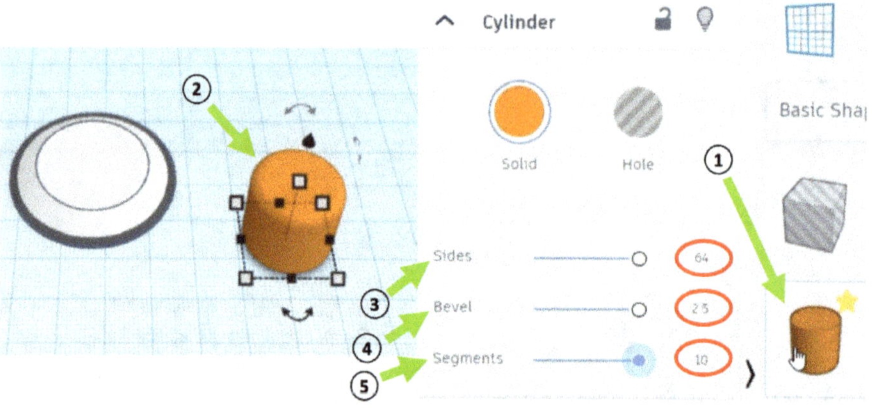

Now we can change the dimensions to 5 mm each for the width and length and 50 mm for the height of the cylindrical body.

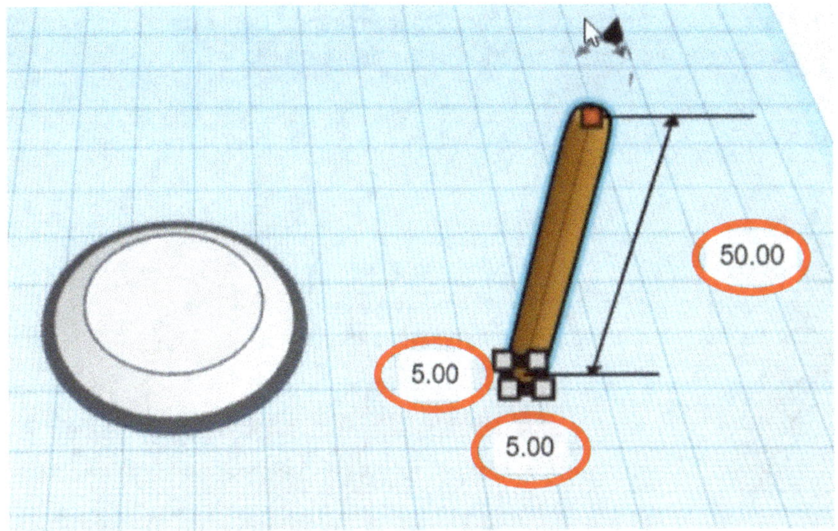

The second part of the linkage will consist of a cross, which will be placed at the top of the bar we have just created. To create the first strut for the cross, we select a cube ① as the basic shape. We change its length to 45 mm, its width to 2 mm and its height to 1 mm ②-④.

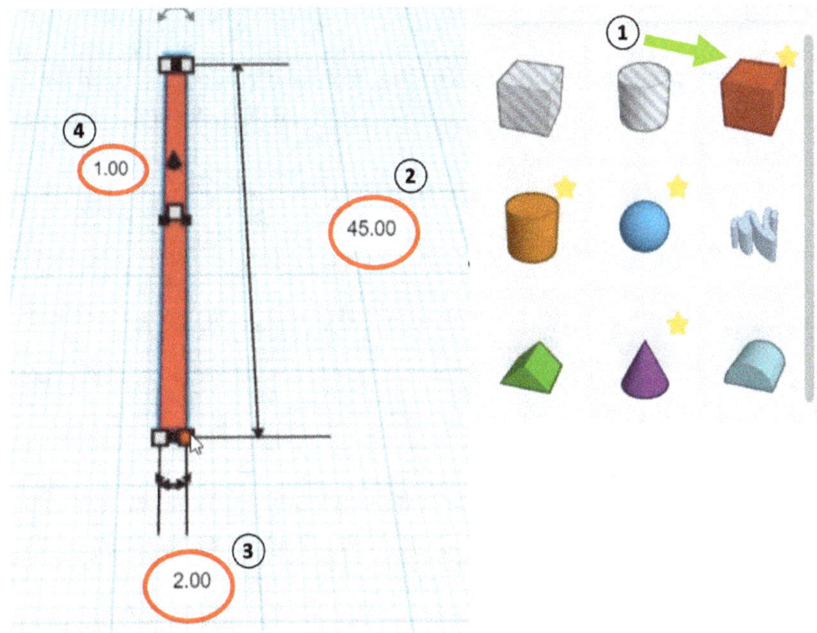

We create the second strut by duplication (command: "Duplicate and repeat") ①-② and by a subsequent 90° rotation of the duplicate ③.

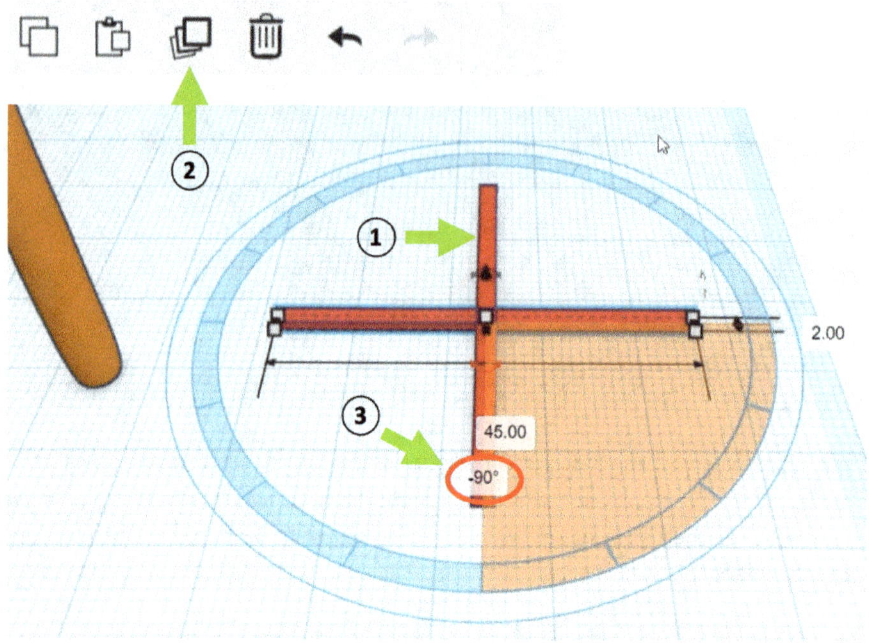

The next step is to change the colors of the struts and group the individual struts into a cross. For both actions, the objects ① must be selected. Then we can perform the actions ②-④.

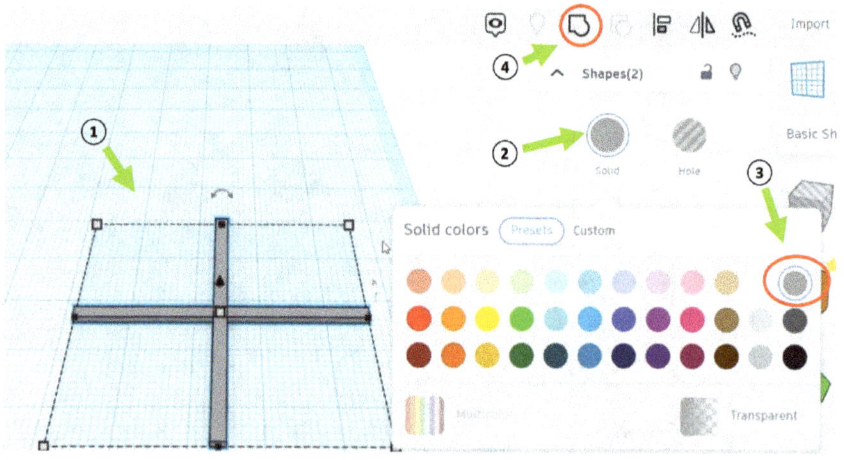

After that, we can assemble the cross and the vertical bar. We do this with the command "Align" ②-⑤ after selecting the objects ①.

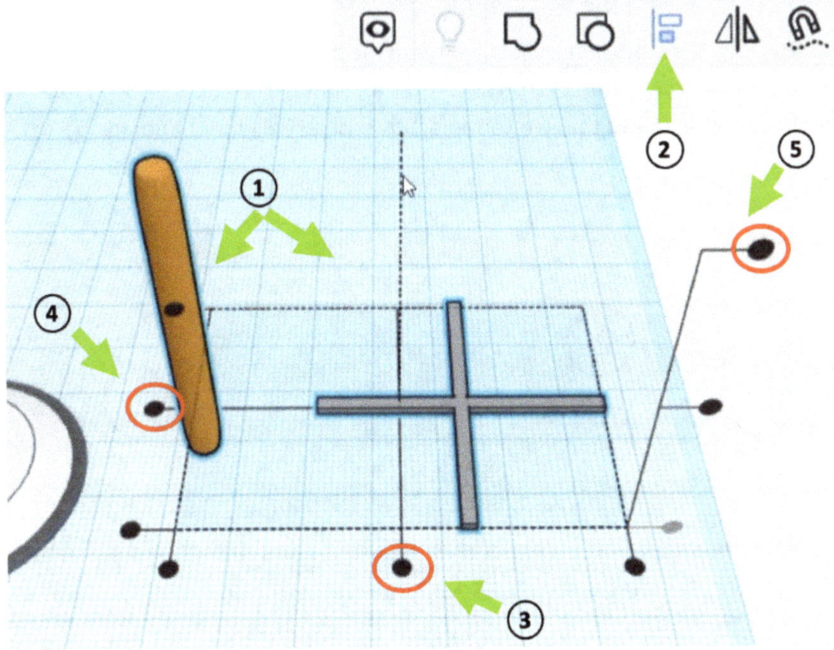

Of course, we also want our lampshade to have a light bulb. So that we don't have to construct it separately, we search for the term "bulb" ① in the Shape Library and drag and drop the bulb ② onto our work plane.

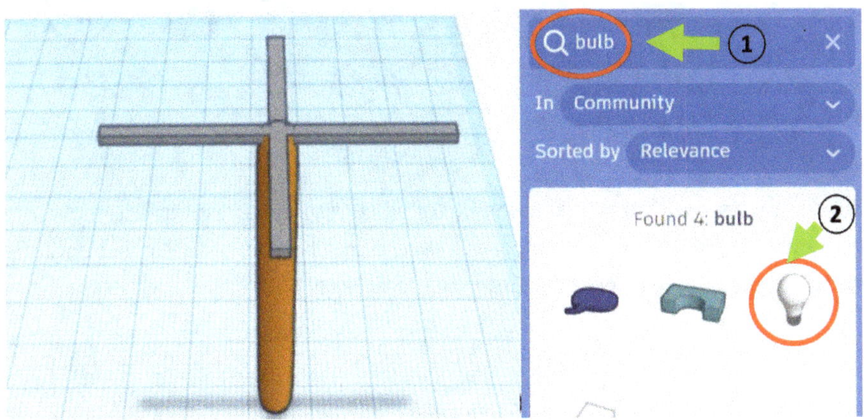

The bulb is huge compared to our other objects. We change that by choosing 7 mm for the width and length of the bulb and 10 mm for the height. Changing the dimensions works the same for this object as it does for all the other objects.

To make sure that the light bulb is centered on the cross of the rod, we select all objects and use the command "Align". After activating the command ①, we first click on the cross ② so that we can select the correct alignment points ③-⑤.

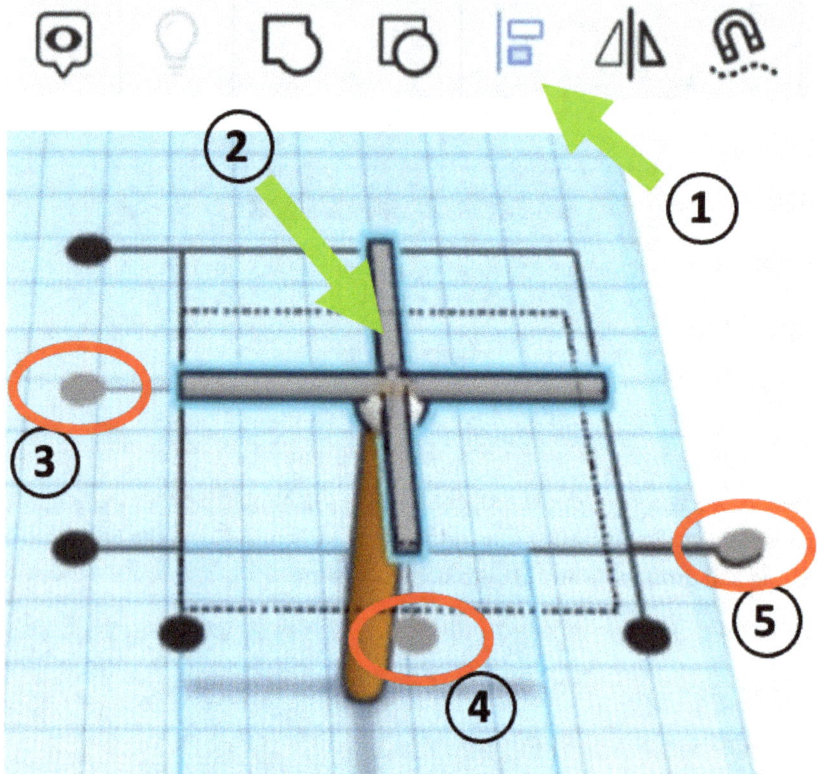

Before we start with the final assembly of all components, we have to move the bulb up a bit. To do this, we simply pull on the small arrow of the object until the socket of the bulb just remains hidden in the linkage.

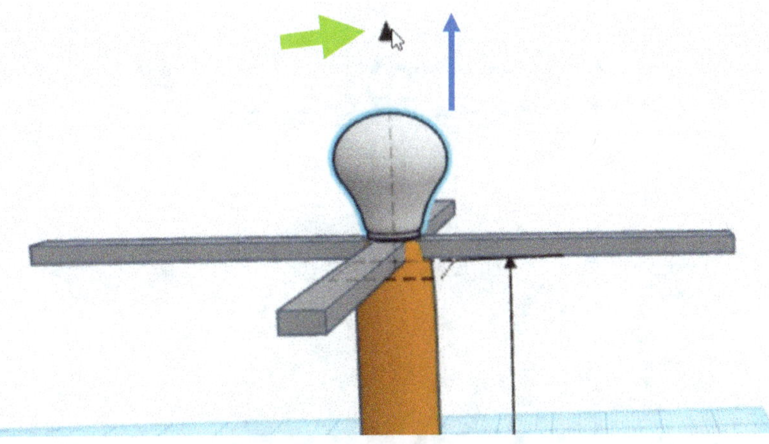

Now, as said, we can start assembling and we are almost at the end of the first project. In the first step, we mark the base as well as the linkage including the bulb and use the command "Align" with the shown alignment points to get the correct positioning.

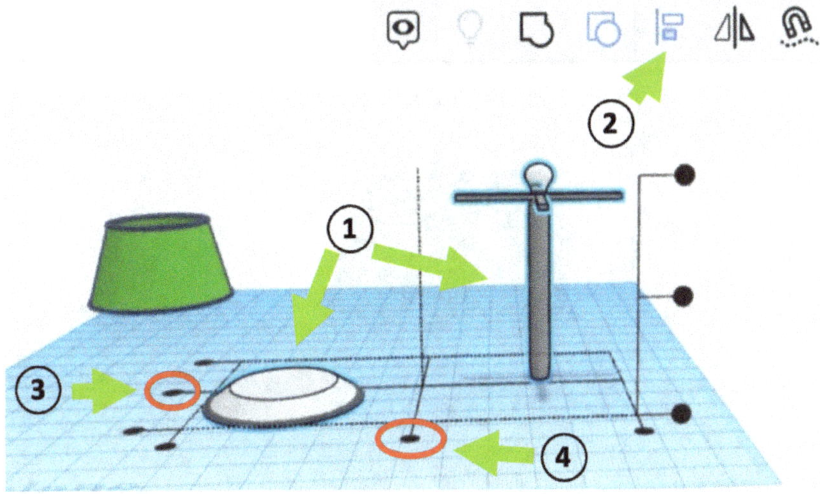

In the second step, we take the lampshade out of the corner and position it in the same way with the rest of the objects. For this, we will use the alignment points shown (command: "Align").

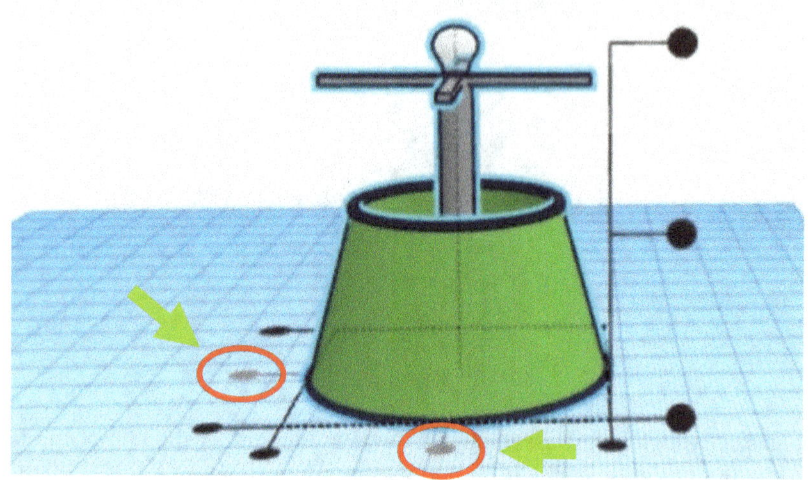

In the last step, we pull the lampshade up to its final position by the small arrow of the object. We pull until the rod is just no longer visible. Then the position is perfect!

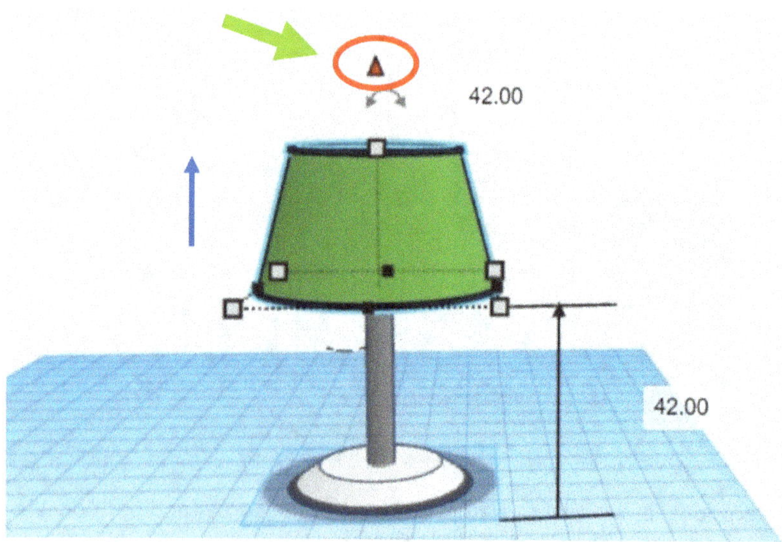

Well done! Now we have completed the first project. I'm glad you stuck with it to the end. Now it's time to move on to the next project, which is a bit more complicated. But don't worry, together we can do it!

Chapter 3 | 3D Model Project 2: Bicycle

Our second project in this course is to be a 3D model of a bicycle. The bike should look like this, and you can copy the project to your account at the following link:

https://tinyurl.com/mr28za59

3.1 The front wheel of the bicycle

After creating a new project for the bike, in this chapter we will first start with the construction of the front wheel. We will need three steps for the creation.

In the first step we create the rim including the tire, in the second step the hub and in the third step the individual spokes. The outer part of the rim and the tire consist of only one body in our simplified model. For this purpose, we select the cylindrical body "Tube" ② from the shape collection "Basic Shapes" ①.

We place this body on the work plane using drag-and-drop and enlarge it in both directions to approx. 36.24 mm. To do this, click on the body, select a corner point, and enter the dimensions.

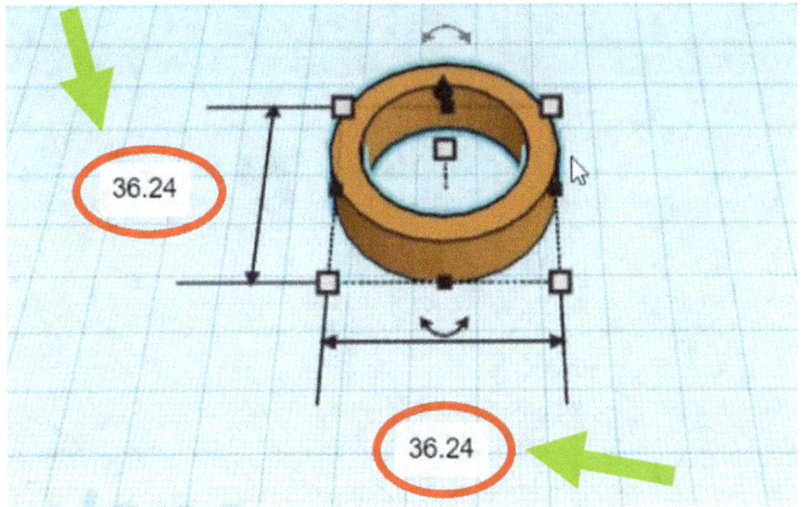

We also change the height of the cylindrical body from 10 mm to approx. 1.81 mm.

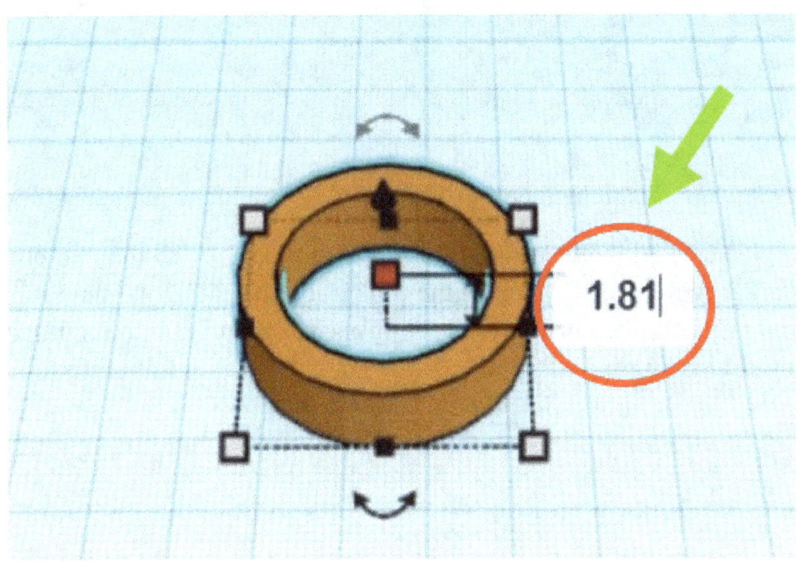

In the 3D object settings, we reduce the wall thickness to 1 mm ① and increase the values for the "Sides", "Bevel" and "Bevel Segments" ② settings to their respective maximum (64, 5, 10). In addition, we change the color to black ③.

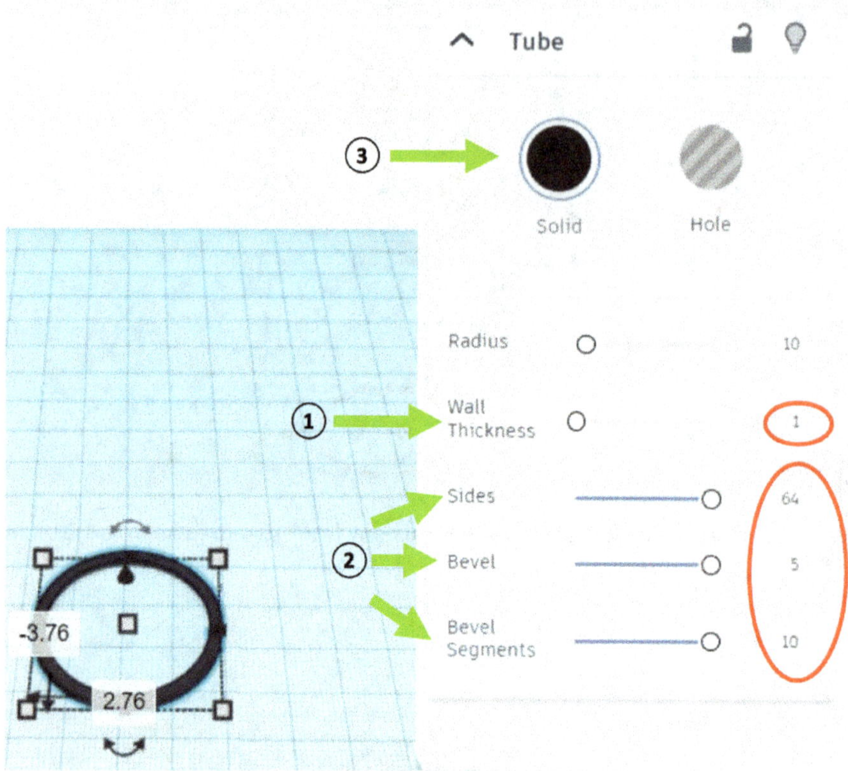

Now we come to the construction of the wheel hub. To do this, we place a cylindrical body ① on any area of the work plane and change its dimensions by clicking on its corner points. For the sides we need 5.38 mm ② each, for the height we need 2 mm ③.

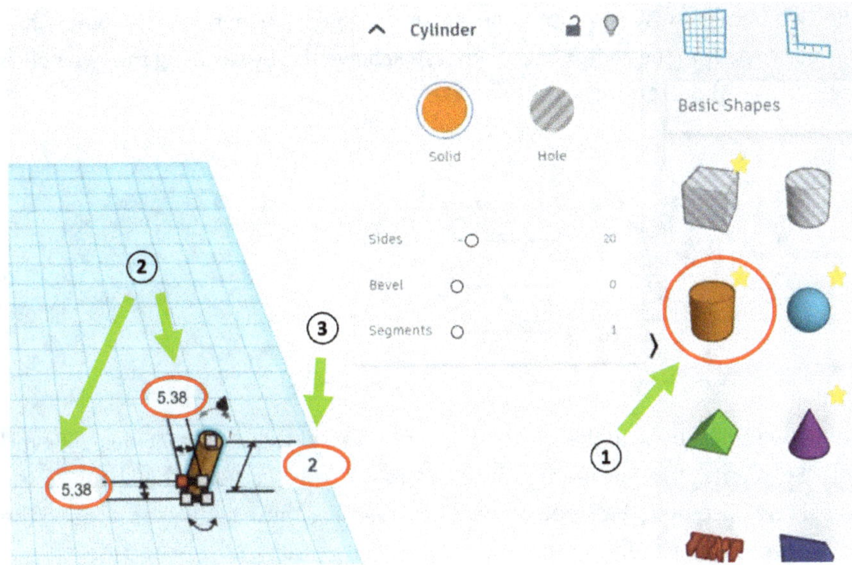

Next, we align the two bodies to each other by spanning a rectangle ① with the left mouse button pressed, selecting the command "Align" ②, or pressing the "L" key.

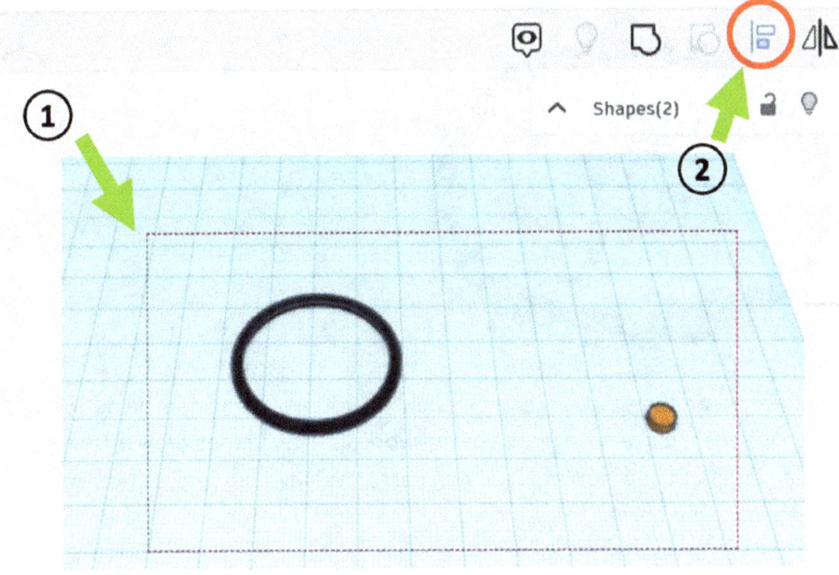

The two bodies must be placed concentrically to each other, i.e., the wheel hub must sit exactly in the center of the rim. We achieve this by selecting the two points shown ①-② one after the other.

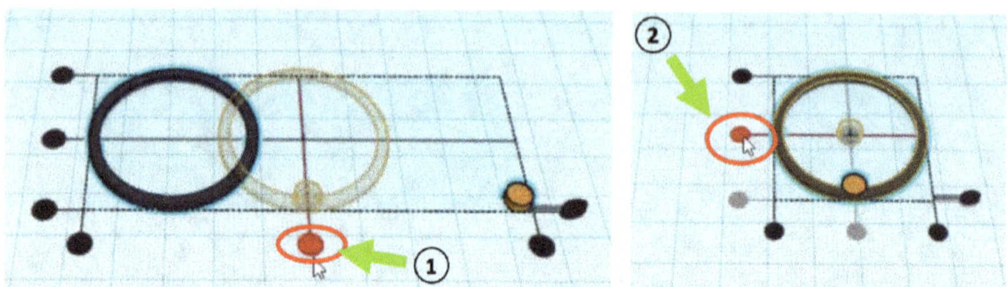

Before we continue with the spokes of the rim, we set the settings "Sides", "Bevel" and "Segments" to their maximum values (64, 2.5, 10), so that the shape of the wheel hub becomes a bit smoother and rounder. For these settings to appear, the body must be selected.

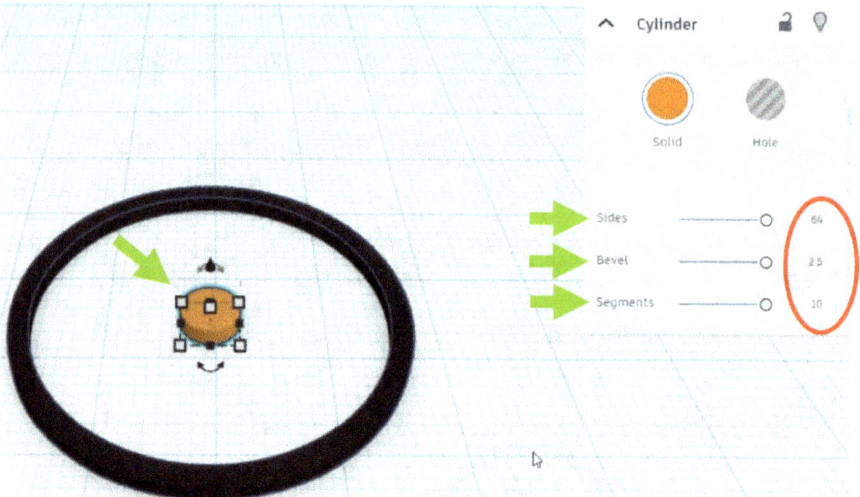

Now we create the first spoke of the rim. To do this, we need a cylindrical body, which we again place on any area of the work surface. Immediately afterward, we change its length and width to 0.20 mm each. We leave the height at the preset 20 mm for the time being.

Then we rotate the body 90° so that it floats horizontally.

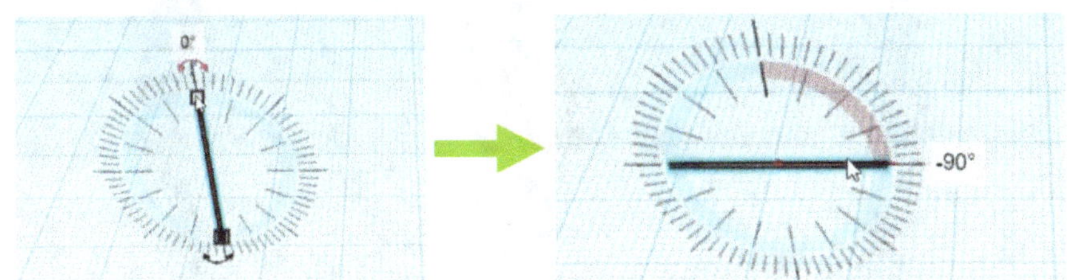

Then we move the body so that it hovers approximately in the center above the other two bodies. For further positioning, we select all three bodies and use the command "Align". After selecting the command, we click on the respective alignment points in the order shown.

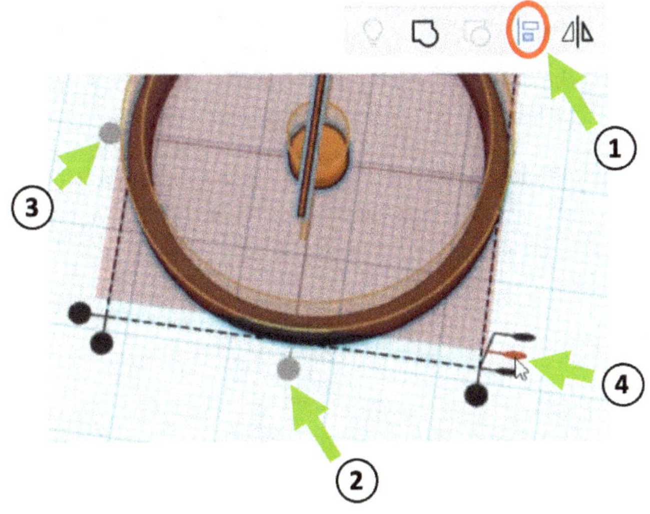

Then we move the bicycle spoke in the direction of the green arrow by using the arrow keys on our keyboard. We also change the length of this first bicycle spoke to 17 mm.

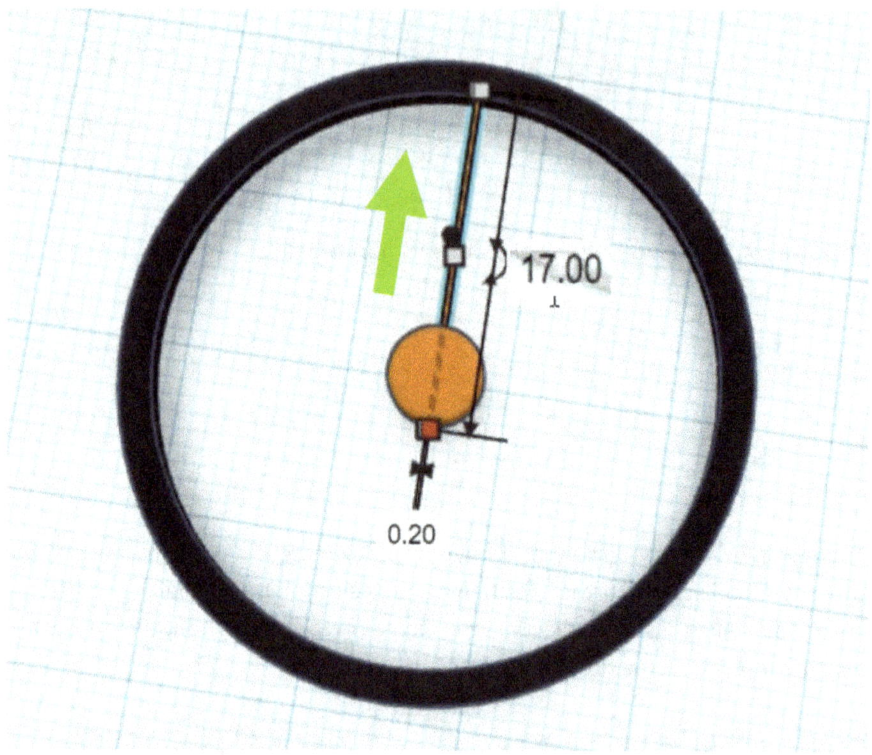

After we have marked the hub and the spoke of the rim ①, we press the "L" key or alternatively select the "Align" command from the menu bar.

We do this to define the position of the bicycle spoke on the outside of the wheel hub in this step. To do this, we first click on the wheel hub ② and then select the point shown ③ for positioning.

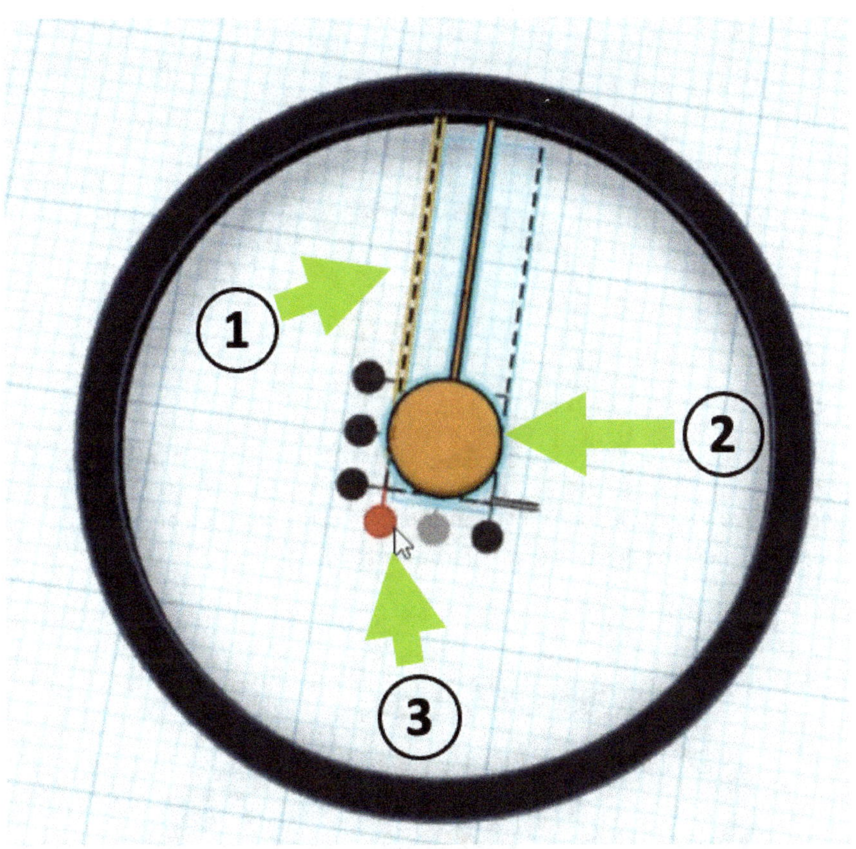

Before we can create a pattern for all the remaining bicycle spokes, we need another identical spoke, which we create after selecting the body by clicking on the "Duplicate and repeat" command from the menu bar in the upper-left corner.

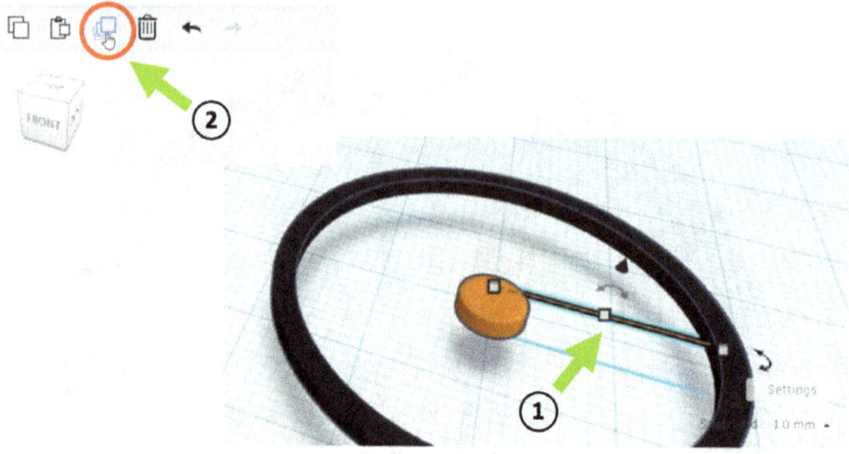

Using the arrow keys, we then move the duplicate in the direction of the red arrows to approximately the position shown (green arrow).

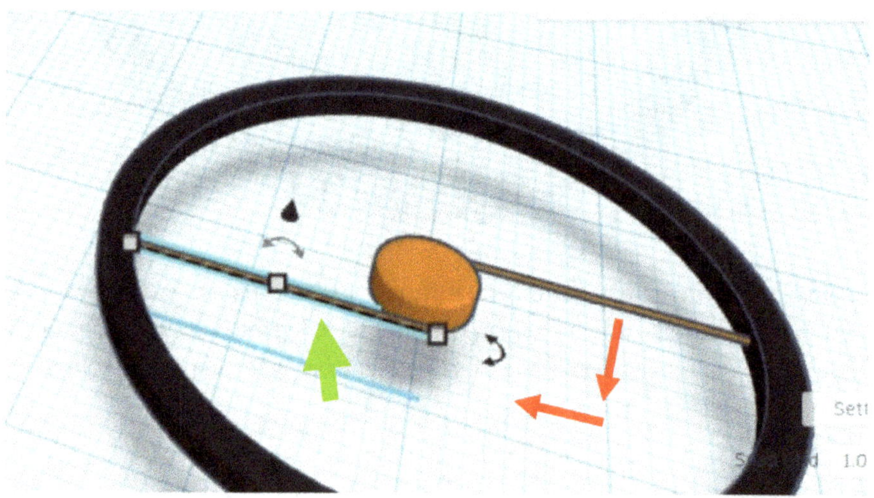

For the exact position, we mark the wheel hub and the bicycle spoke (① and ②) and press the "L" key to call the "Align" command. We use the same procedure here as before for the first bicycle spoke. Therefore, we then click on the wheel hub ② and select the displayed positioning point ③.

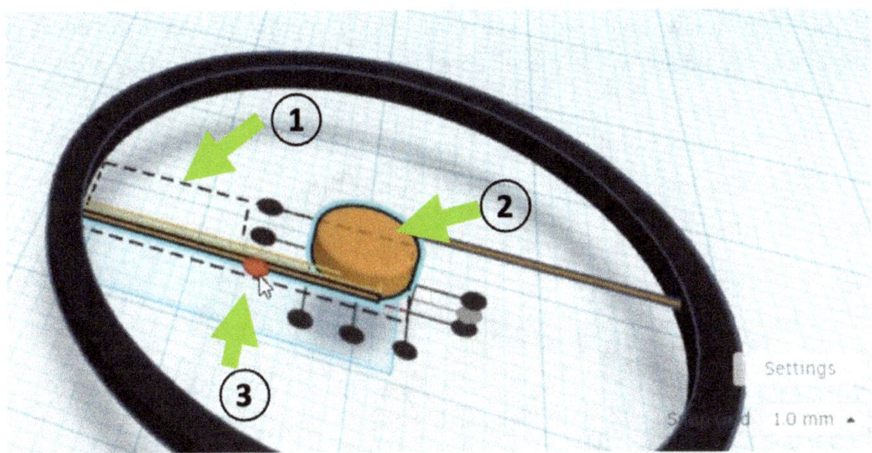

Then we move the bicycle spoke a little in the direction of the tire / rim so that we get approximately the following result. Also check the opposite bicycle spoke, which should be positioned similarly.

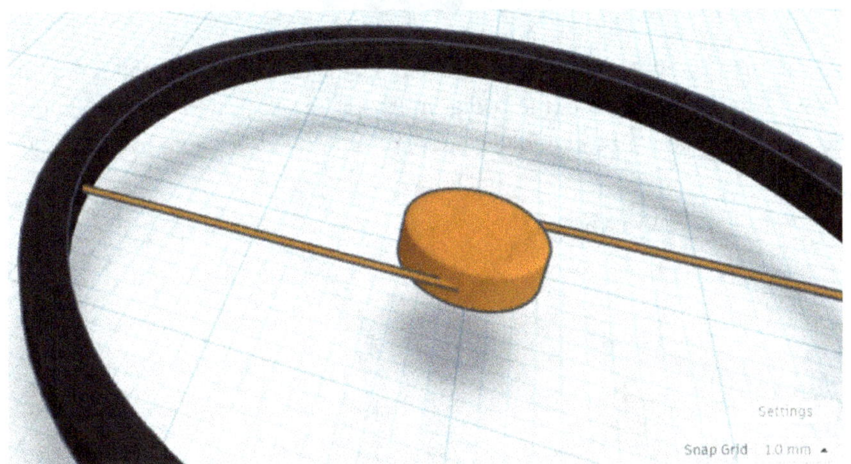

We can now create all the other bicycle spokes in a quick and easy way. Stop for a moment and think about how we could do this.

-- Solution follows here --

We select both bicycle spokes by simply clicking on them ① (while holding down the Shift key) and then select the command "Duplicate and repeat" ② again. To activate this command, we could alternatively simply use the key combination

"CTRL+D". By the way, you won't see much after executing the command because the duplicated bodies will be placed congruently on the already existing ones.

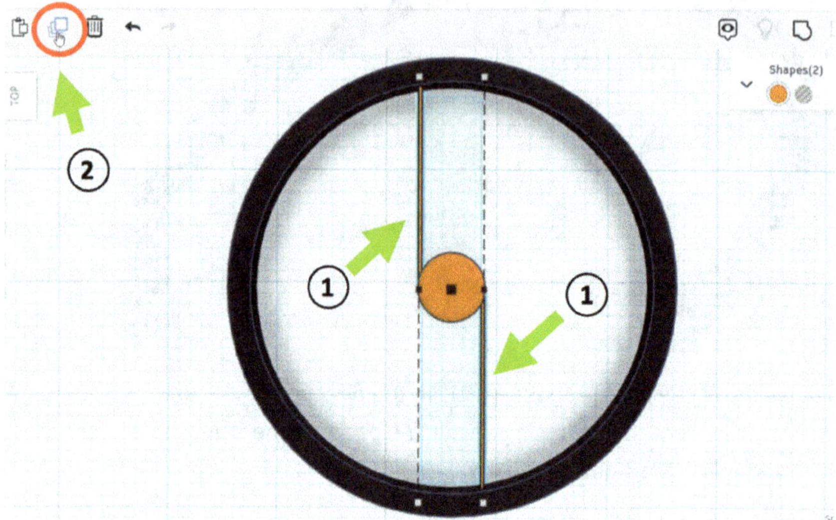

We can then rotate the duplicated elements by clicking on the small red double arrow ① in the lower area (the bodies must still be selected for this) and moving the mouse so that we get the following representation. We rotate by 22.5° ②.

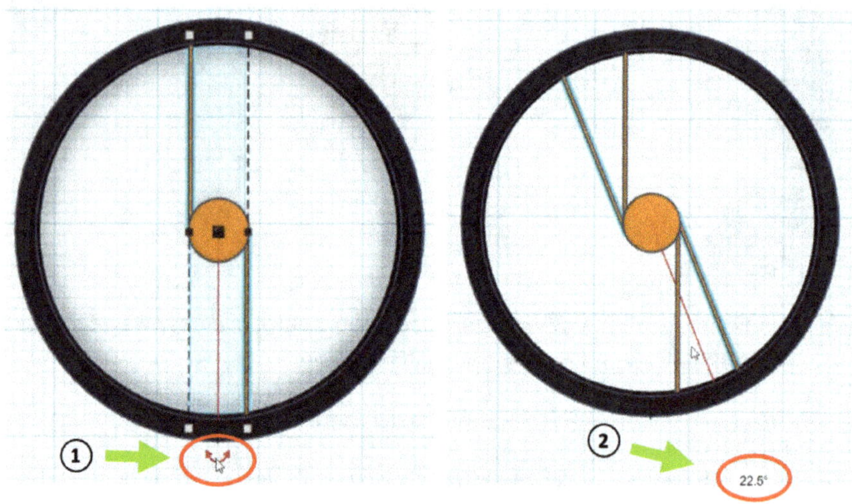

If we then click on the "Duplicate and Repeat" command six times in a row – without clicking on anything else beforehand – the remaining spokes will automatically be placed in the correct orientation. Almost magical!

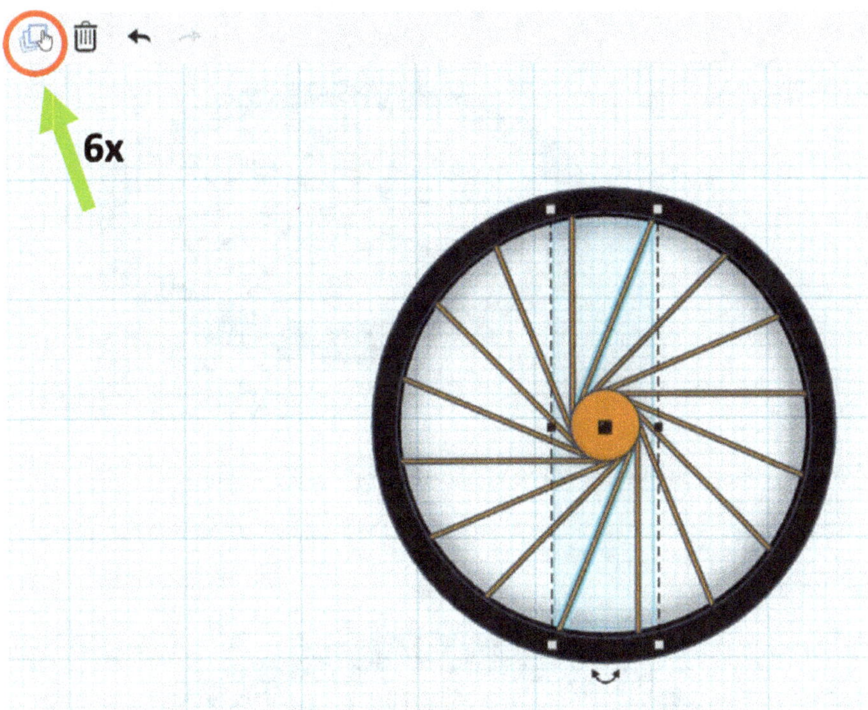

We then want to add a front fork mount to our wheel hub. We do this by clicking on the hub ① and selecting the command "Duplicate and repeat" ②. Furthermore, we click on a corner point of the duplicated body and enter 3.62 mm as the dimension ③.

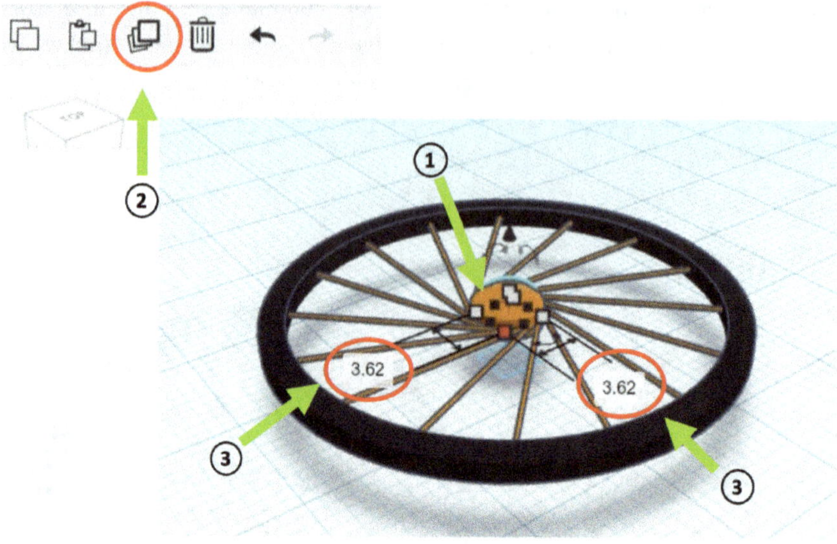

We also change the height of the duplicated body to 7.25 mm.

So that the created body is centered in the plane of the front wheel, we select all the bodies created so far and use the command "Align" ①. We click on the alignment point shown ②.

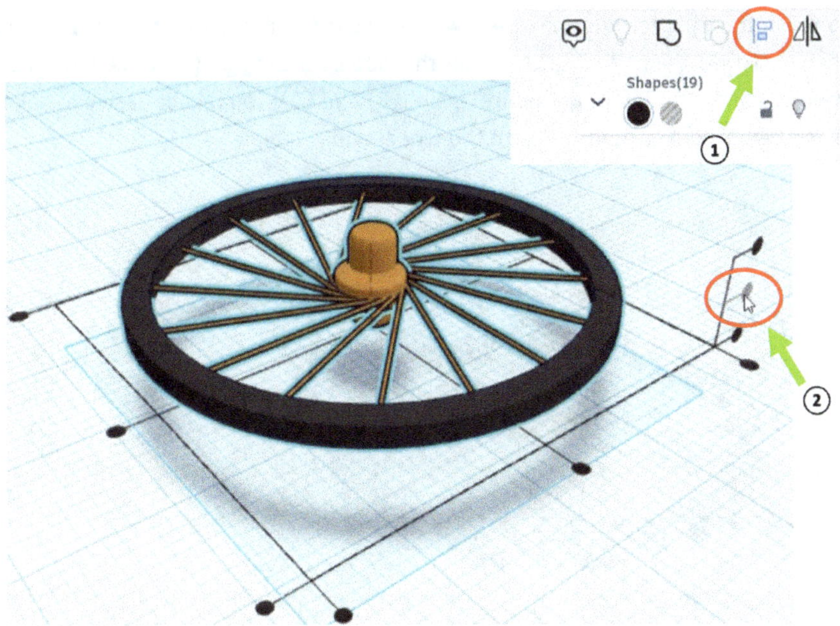

Then we also need to align the duplicated object centrally to the wheel hub itself. We do this by selecting the two orange bodies, pressing the "L" key (or ①) and then clicking on the alignment points shown (② and ③) one after the other. For better display, all other bodies are hidden here (by clicking on the light bulb icon).

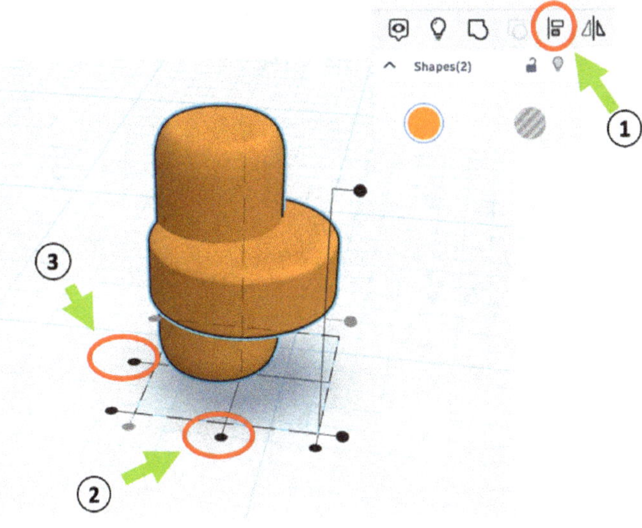

To finish the chapter, we make a few color adjustments and then group all the objects. To do this, I first showed all the bodies again ① (no object must be selected) and then hid only the tire again (② and ③) to make it easier to select all the wheel spokes together with the wheel hub.

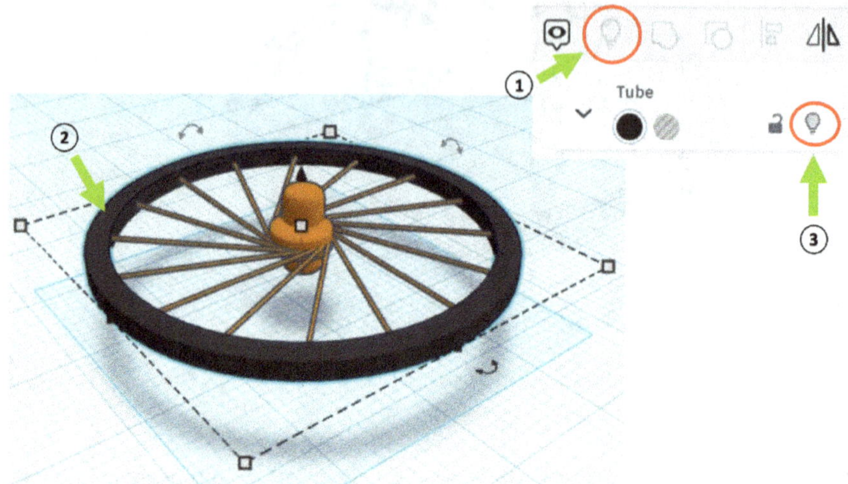

This leaves only the wheel spokes and the wheel hub visible. We select all objects and choose a gray color in the settings.

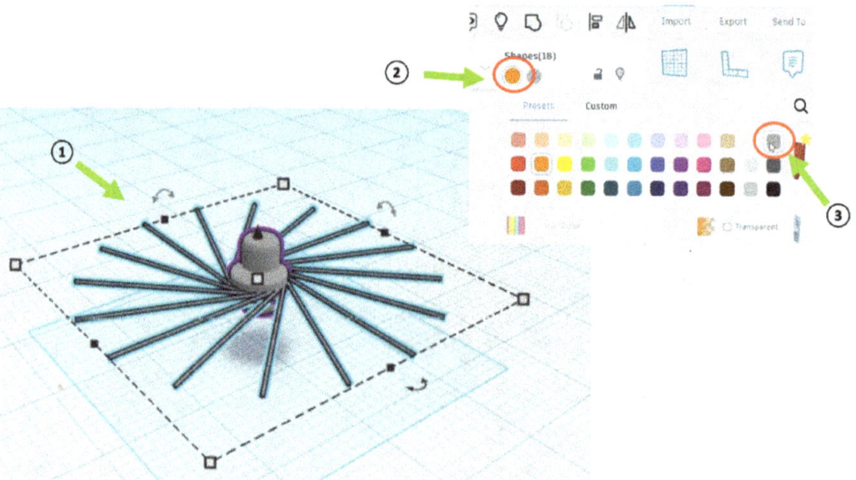

You can also pick something more colorful or, for example, color the wheel hub black, as I did in the next step (① and ②).

Then briefly click on the work plane to finish selecting objects. Afterwards I showed the rim / tire again by clicking on the command "Show all" ③. For this command, you can alternatively press the key combination "CTRL+SHIFT+H".

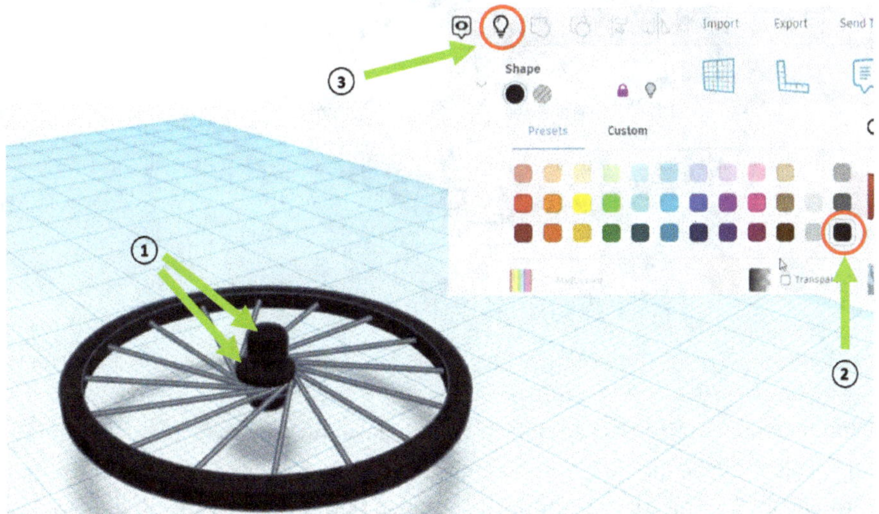

To combine all the bodies created so far into one front wheel, we select all the objects ① and choose the command "Group" ②. Alternatively, you could also use the key combination "CTRL+G".

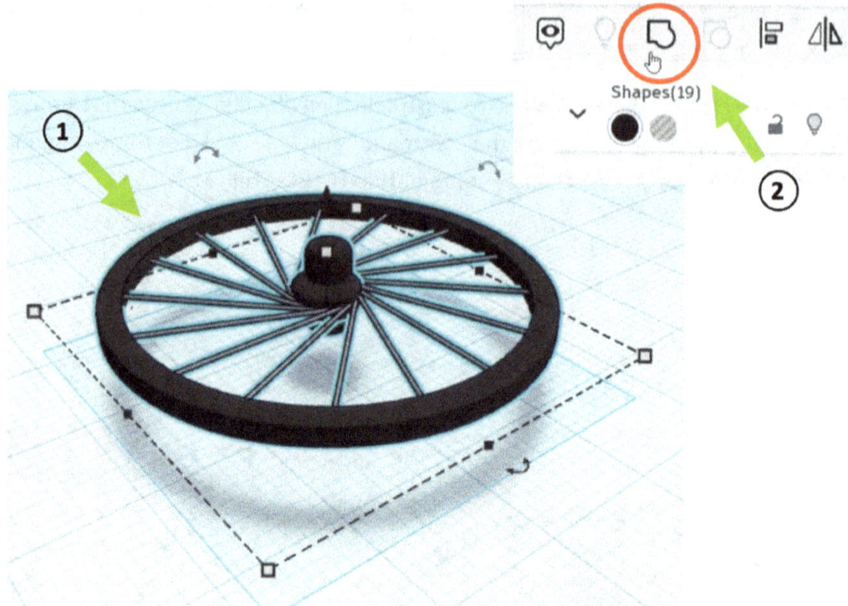

You may now notice that all objects are displayed in only one color. In order for the colors to be displayed separately again, we have to activate the option "Multicolor" in the color settings. The grouped object must be selected.

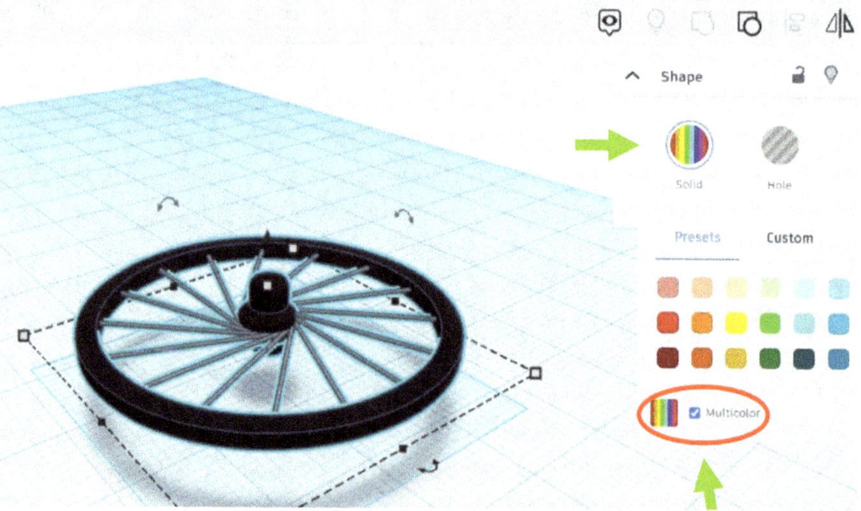

3.2 The front fork of the bicycle

In this chapter, we will deal with the front fork of the bicycle. For the creation of the wheel fork, we use a curved pipe as initial geometry, which we can find with the search term "pipe" ① in the shape library of "Tinkercad". We click on the icon with the magnifying glass beforehand to get to the search input.

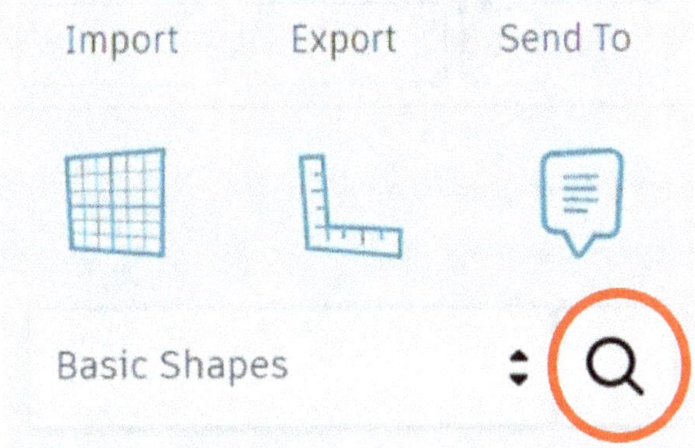

From the search results, select the object that looks a bit like a purple macaroni noodle ② and place it on your workplane using drag-and-drop.

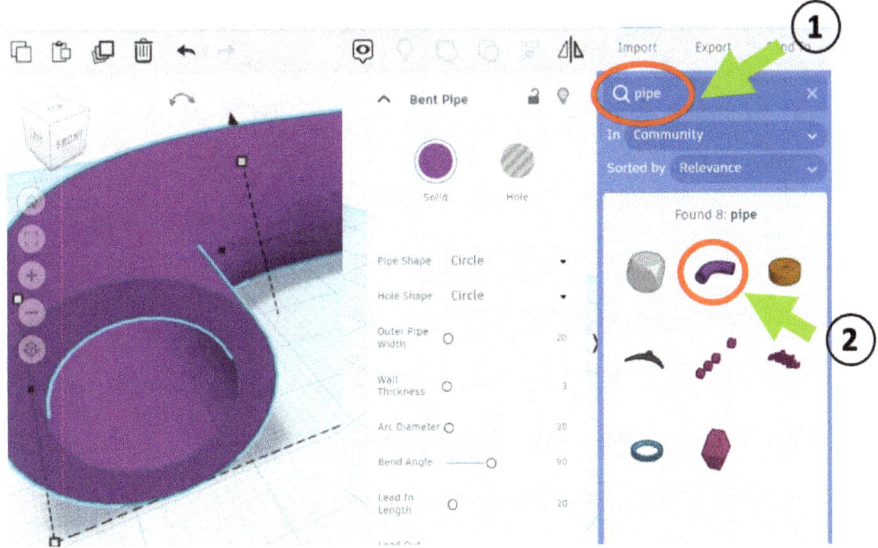

To make the curved tube take the shape of our front fork, we change the preset values as follows (circled in red; from top to bottom: 2, 99, 10, 180, 50, 50).

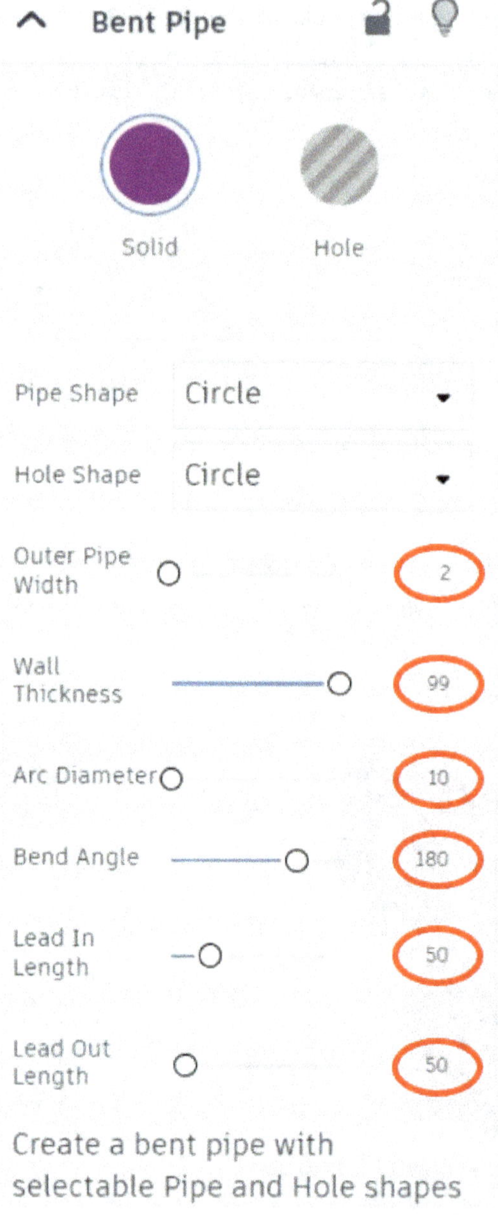

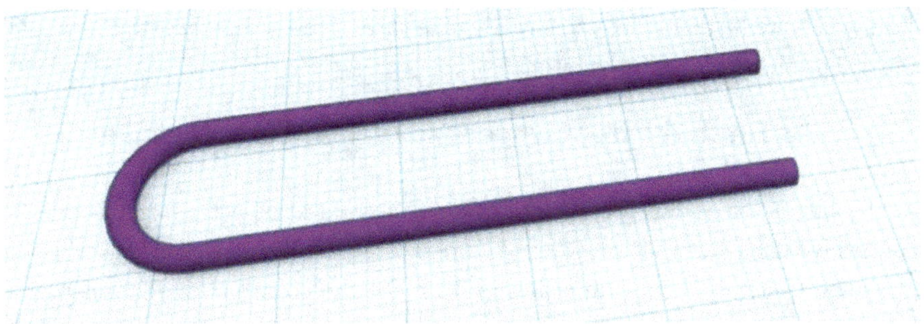

Now, the front fork is still too long and too wide for our bike. Therefore, in the next step, we change the width dimension to 7.25 mm and the length dimension to 27.18 mm. For this, I clicked on one of the corner points before.

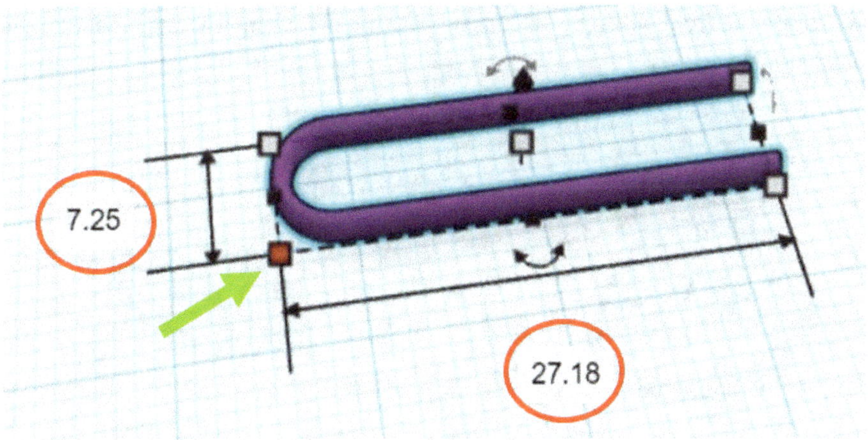

We also change the height of the geometry to 1.81 mm.

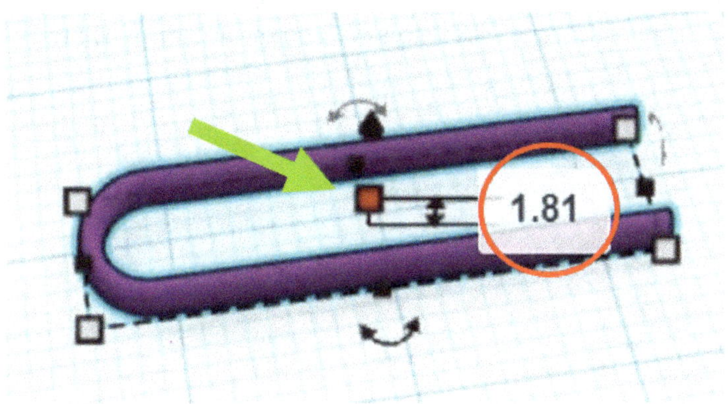

That was quite fast, now we can already take care of the assembly with the wheel. We will do that in the next chapter.

3.3 Finish the front wheel and rear wheel of the bike

At the beginning of the project, we called the created object a front wheel. Of course, we can use this front wheel as a rear wheel at the same time, for this we just need to create a copy. In order not to make the construction more complex than necessary, this also applies to the rear fork, which we will create from two front forks. In the next steps, we will first create the rear wheel with the rear fork. Here's how we do that.

In the first step, we connect the wheel fork to the wheel hub. To accomplish this, we rotate the front wheel by 90° by selecting the object and clicking on one of the small double arrows.

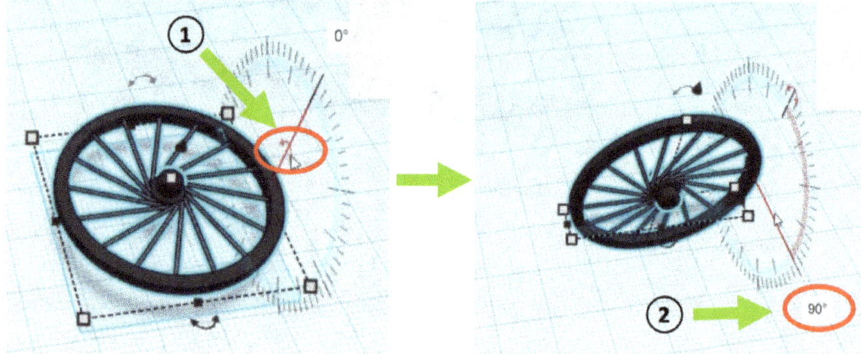

To position the wheel fork, we select both objects, press the "L" key – this selects the "Align" command – and click successively on the alignment points shown.

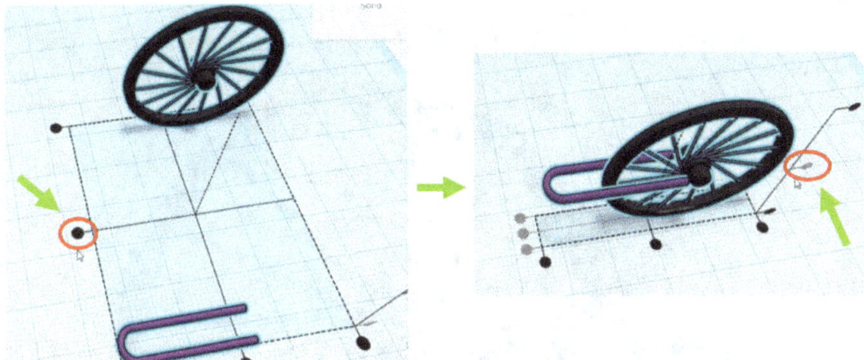

Then we push the wheel fork a bit more towards the wheel hub so that the wheel fork is roughly centered in the wheel hub.

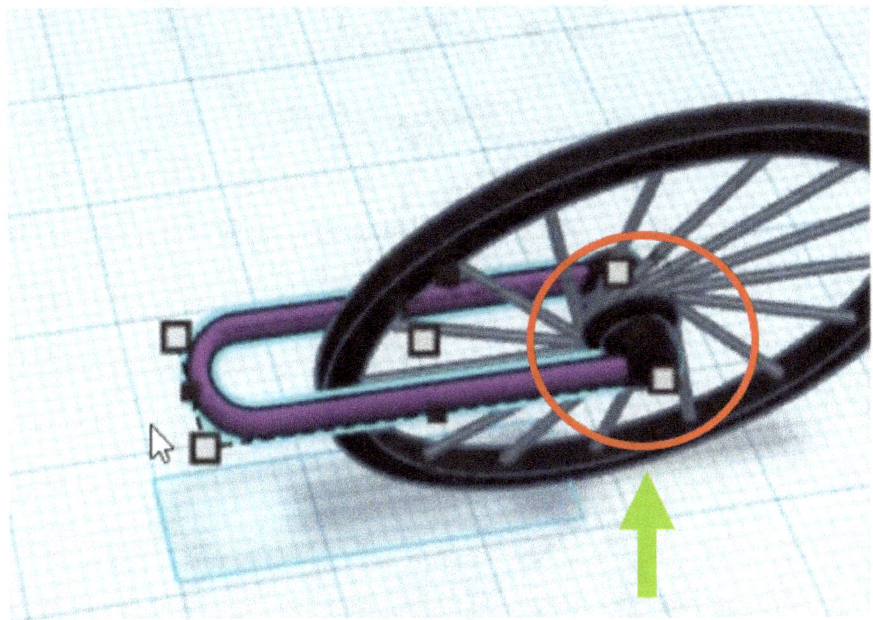

To create the second part of the rear fork, we simply copy the curved tube by selecting it and pressing "CTRL+D" (shortcut for "Duplicate and repeat"). We then rotate the duplicated object by 45°.

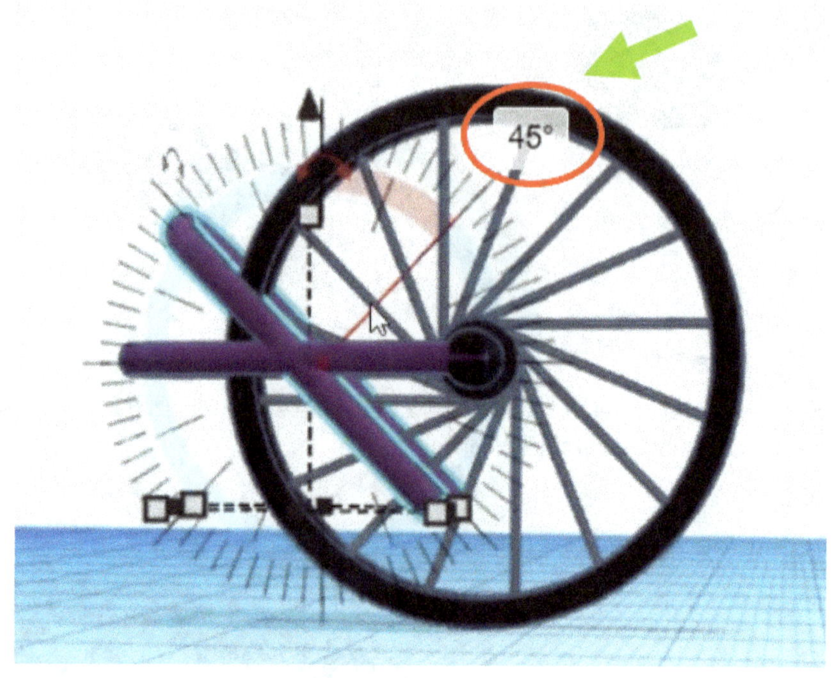

We position the object by moving it up and toward the center so that it sits in the wheel hub approximately as shown.

This object now represents our rear wheel with the rear fork.

To create the front wheel, we select the rear wheel, as well as the lower part of the rear fork (① and ②) and copy these two objects with "CTRL+D".

Immediately afterward, we can move the duplicated objects backwards using the arrow keys on our keyboard ① and shorten the length of the front fork to 22 mm ②.

3.4 Create the bike frame

In this chapter, we will create some struts for the bicycle frame, which we will then connect.

For the first strut, we need a cylindrical element whose lateral dimensions we set to 3.62 mm ① and whose height we increase to 36.25 mm ②. We also set the values for the options "Sides", "Bevel" and "Segments" ③ to their respective maximum (64, 2.5, 10).

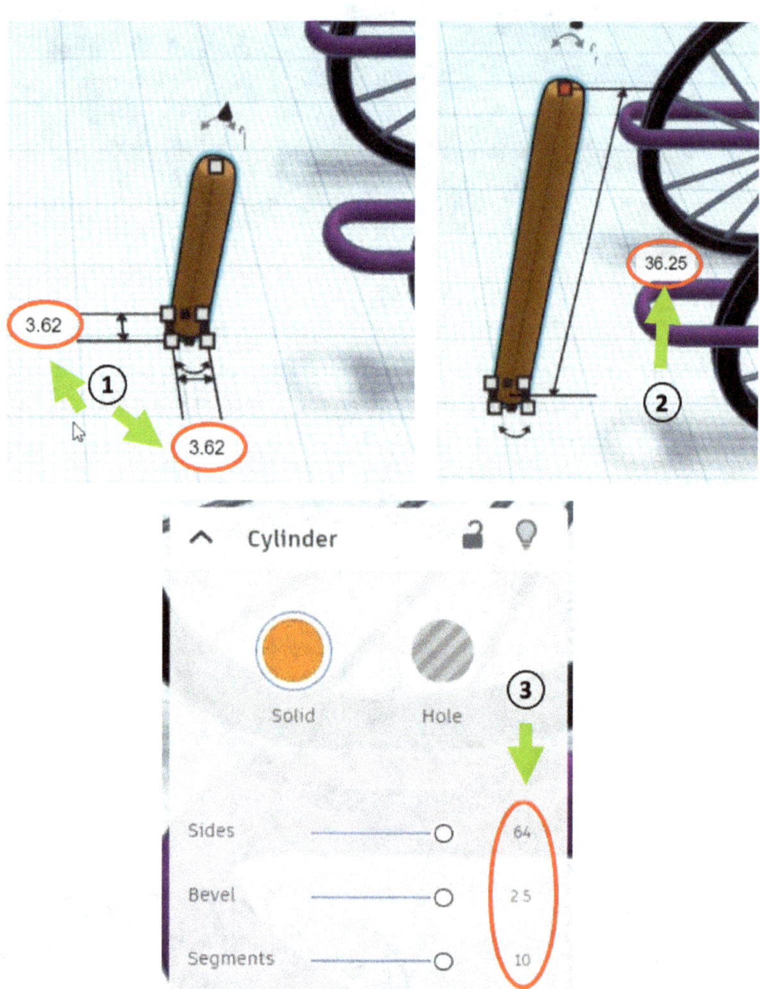

Now we position the strut on the rear fork by selecting the strut and the rear wheel and then pressing the "L" key (short command for "Align"). We select one of the middle alignment points ① and then rotate the strut by 22.5° ②.

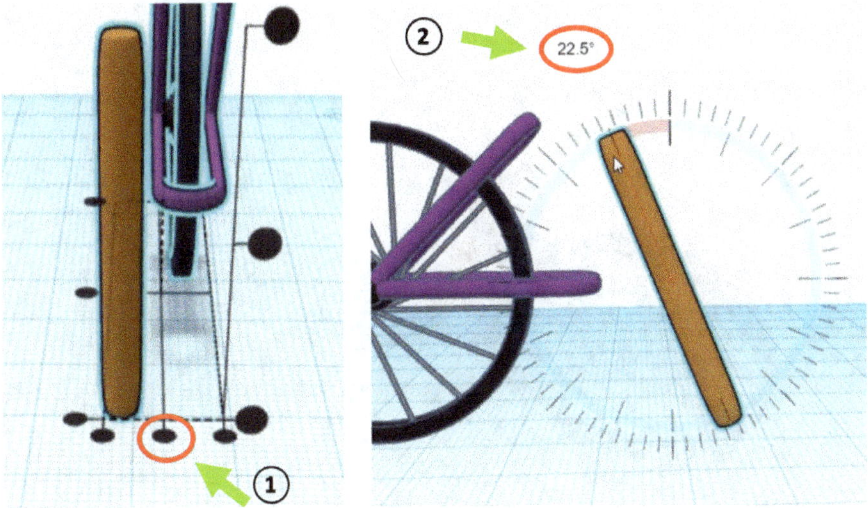

Then we move the strut to the displayed position using the arrow keys on the keyboard or by dragging it with the mouse.

Before we create the next strut, we first use the command "Workplane tool" ①
or press the "W" key as a shortcut. Then we select the upper surface of the strut
②.

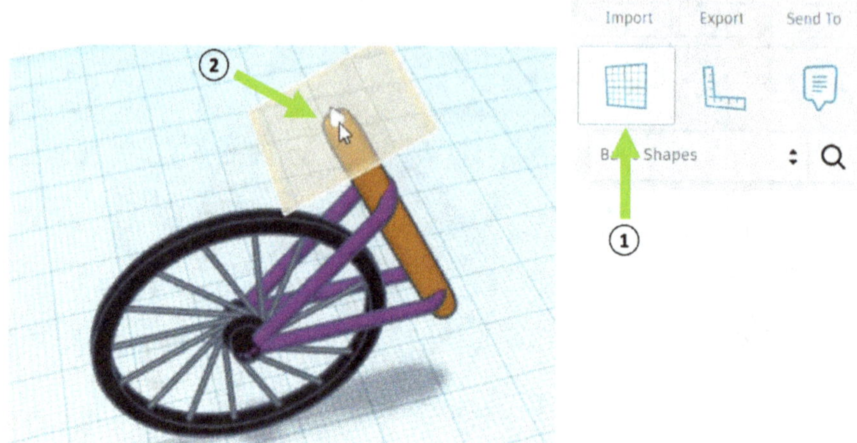

Now our workplane is on the strut. This helps us to be able to position the next
strut, that we create by duplication (shortcut: "CTRL+D"), using the virtual ruler.
We will see how this works in a moment. First follows the duplication and a manual
move, as shown.

After that, we use the virtual ruler, which we can activate with the command "Ruler
tool" ① or by pressing the "R" key (short command). We place the ruler on the

top of the first strut ②. This will cause a two-dimensional scale with dimensions to appear.

In the next step, we change the distance between the two struts to about 41.96 mm by moving the front strut.

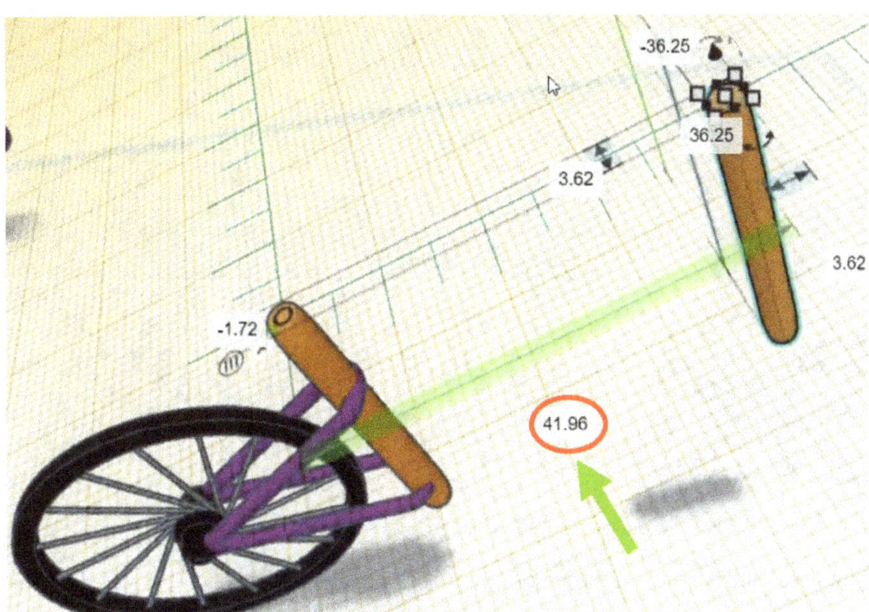

Next, we shorten the front strut to a height of about 10.87 mm.

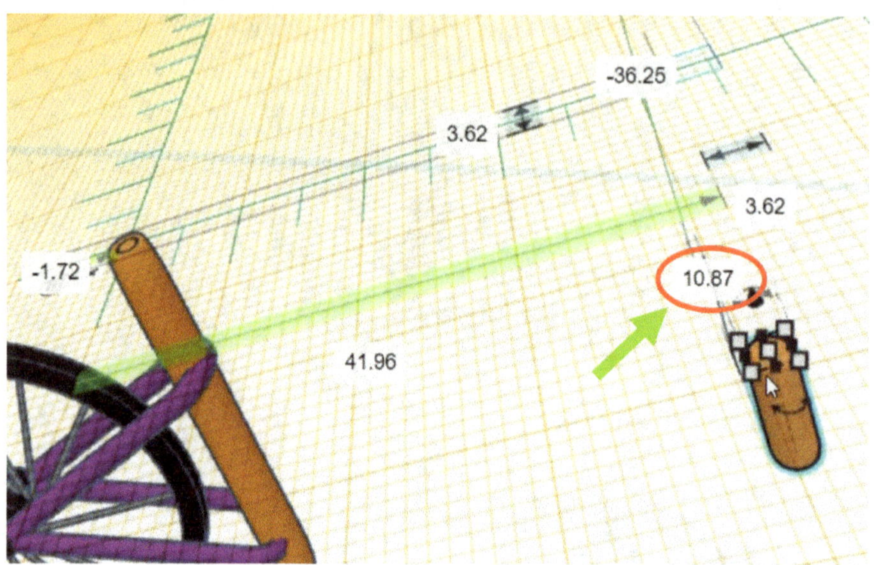

And then we change the vertical position of the strut to -18.12 mm, so that it is placed a little further up.

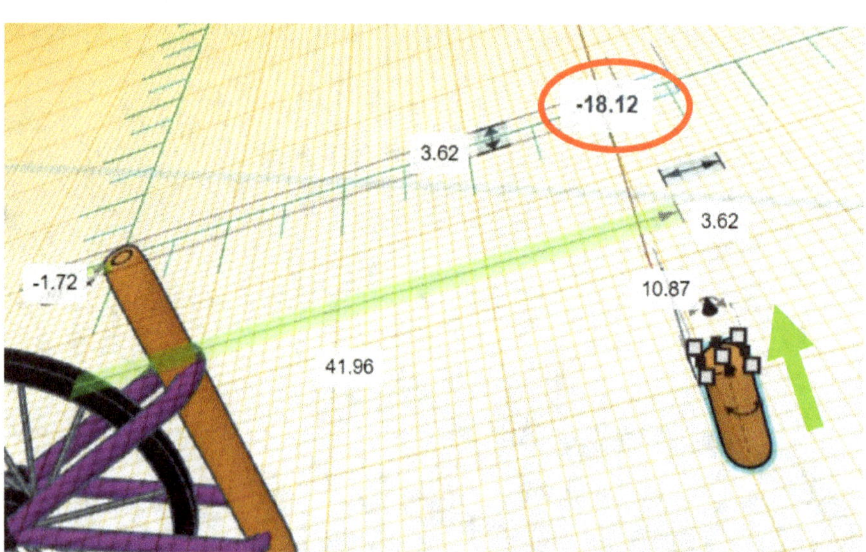

Then we duplicate – using the command: "Duplicate and repeat" – once again the strut ① that we had created at the beginning and rotate it by 90° ②.

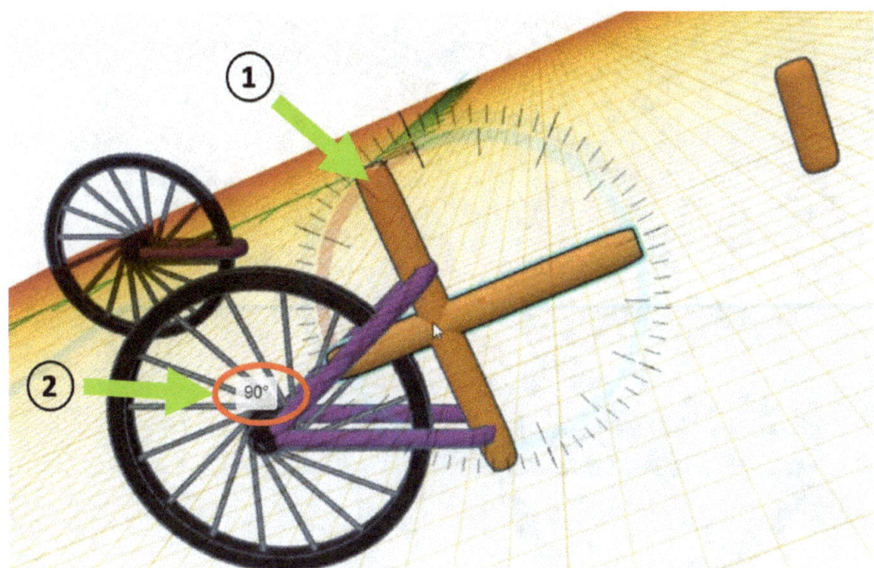

Immediately afterward, we move this strut to the right and upwards and extend it on the right side so that it gets the position shown. We also increase the width from 3.62 mm to 4.00 mm.

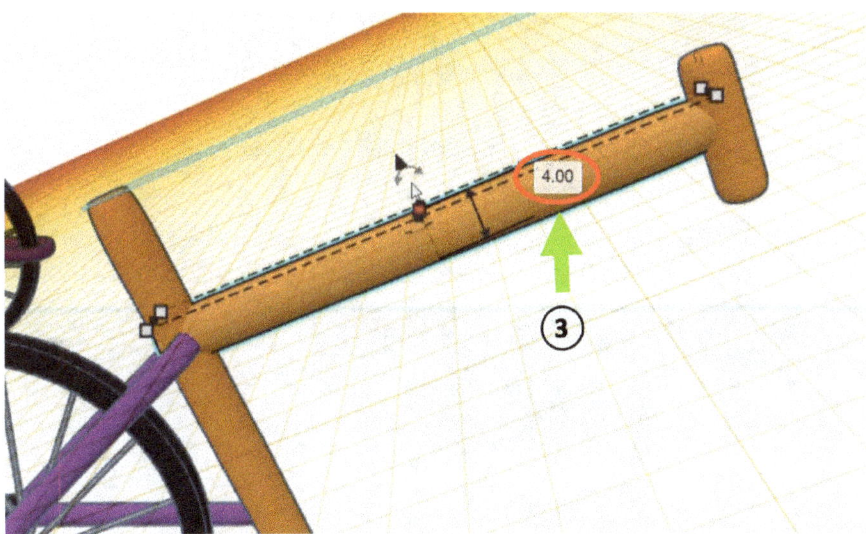

Then we duplicate the horizontal strut ("CTRL+D"), rotate it by 22.5° and move it to the desired position as well.

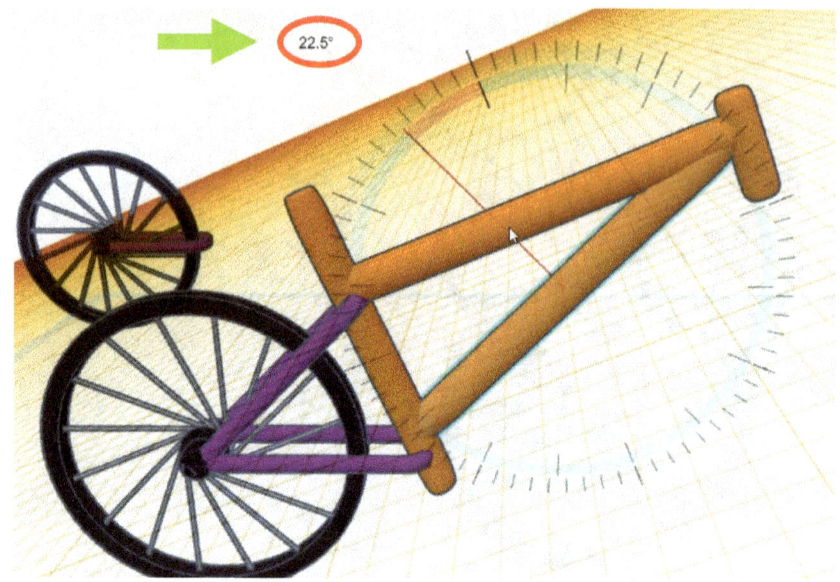

Now the front of the bike is still a little too high, so we rotate it by -10° (select everything beforehand) and then place it on our working plane by pressing the "D" key. The rear wheel should then touch the working plane.

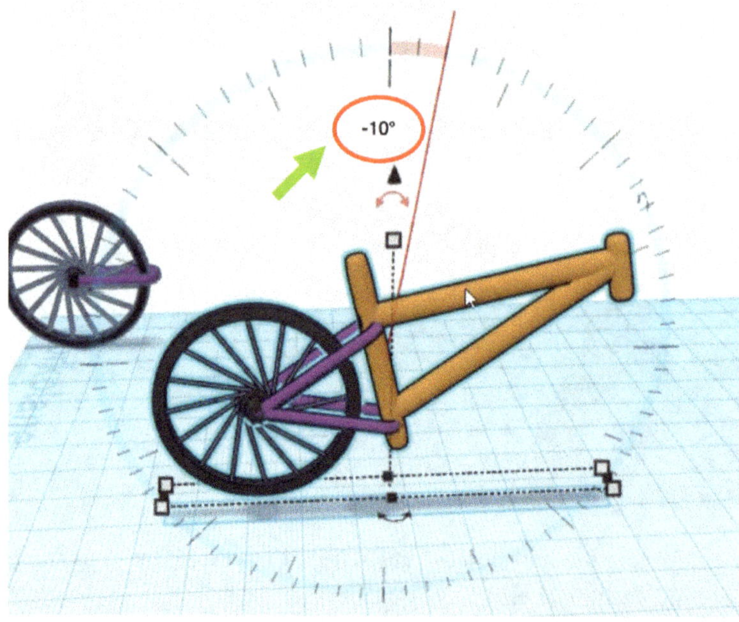

We then move and rotate the front wheel so that the front fork is facing up as shown and the front wheel sits below the bike frame.

With the help of the command "Align" (short command: "L") we make sure that the front wheel is positioned in the center of the bicycle. To do this, first select all objects and then select the alignment point shown.

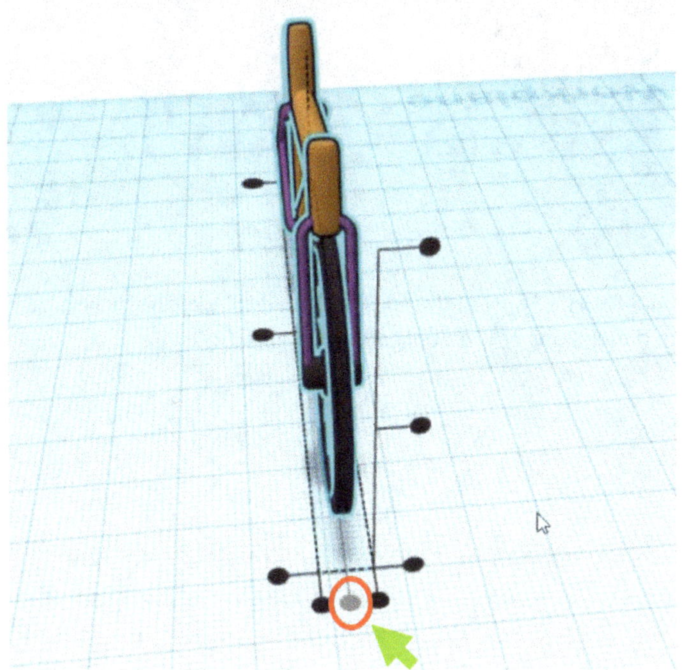

Now we make a few more changes to the front fork so that we can also mount the handlebars on the bike later.

To do this, we place the work plane on the bottom ① of the front fork by using the short command "W" (and a click). Thereafter, we can shorten the fork a bit by dragging it to about 20 mm ②. I have hidden the front wheel for this.

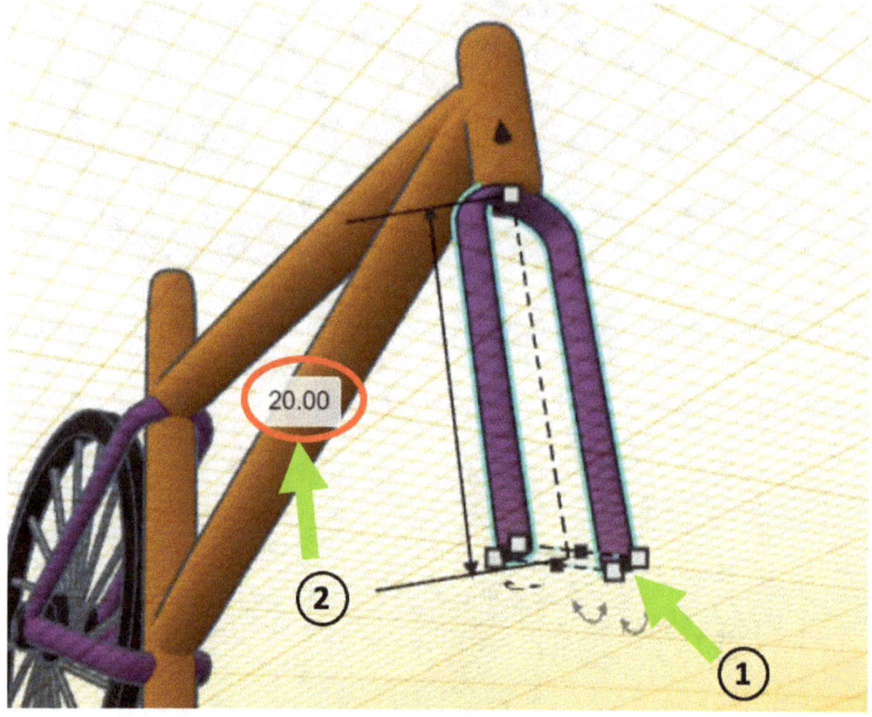

Then we duplicate ("CTRL+D") the so-called head tube of the bicycle frame ① and change the dimensions of the duplicate to 2.5 mm ②.

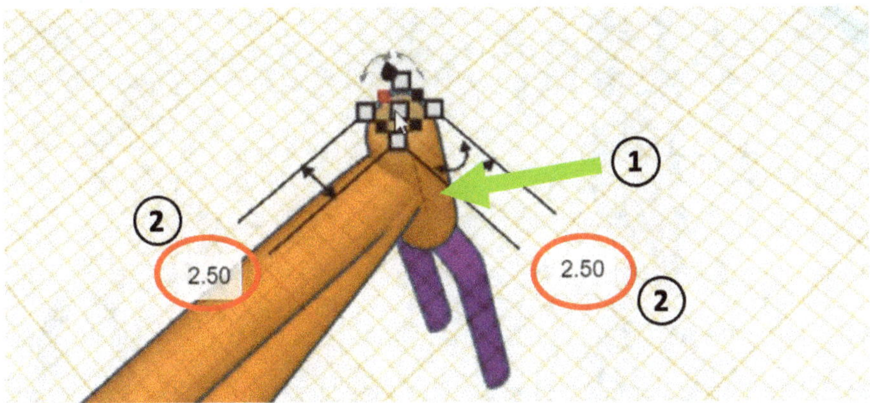

We also change the length of the duplicated object to 14.87 mm.

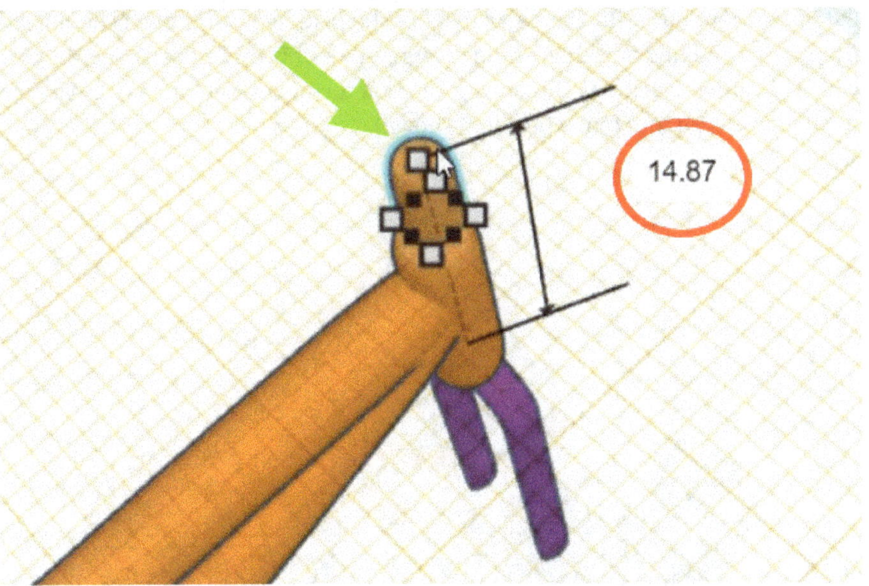

And finally, we make sure that the duplicated object is centered in the head tube. To do this, we select the two objects ①, press the "L" key and click on the alignment points ② and ③ shown. You may have to move the bicycle fork down a bit so that it is positioned as shown.

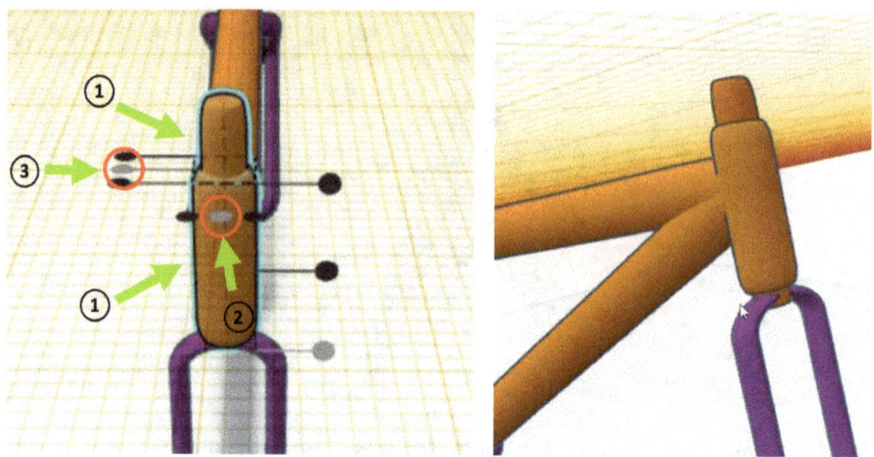

Before we continue with the handlebars of the bike, we can protect the objects from further editing and change the colors. We do this by first selecting the rear wheel ① and then closing the small padlock in the upper-right area ②. We then do the same with the front wheel (not shown).

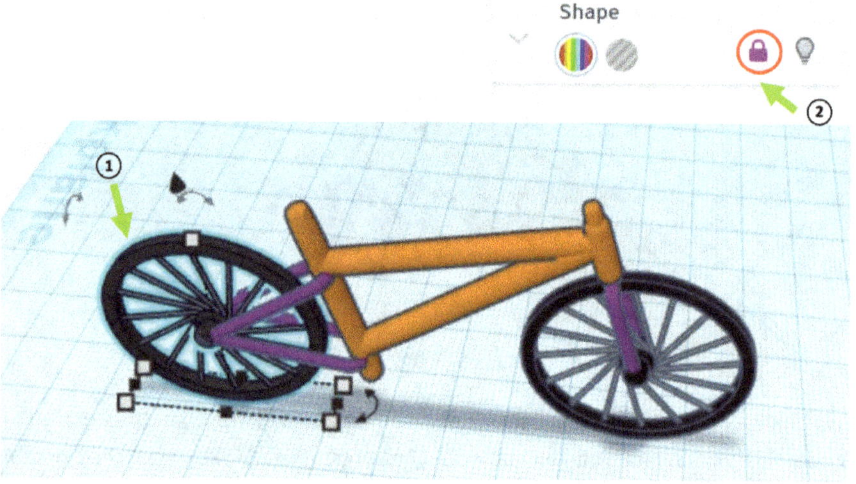

We change the color of the bike frame by selecting all the objects and using a shade that we like.

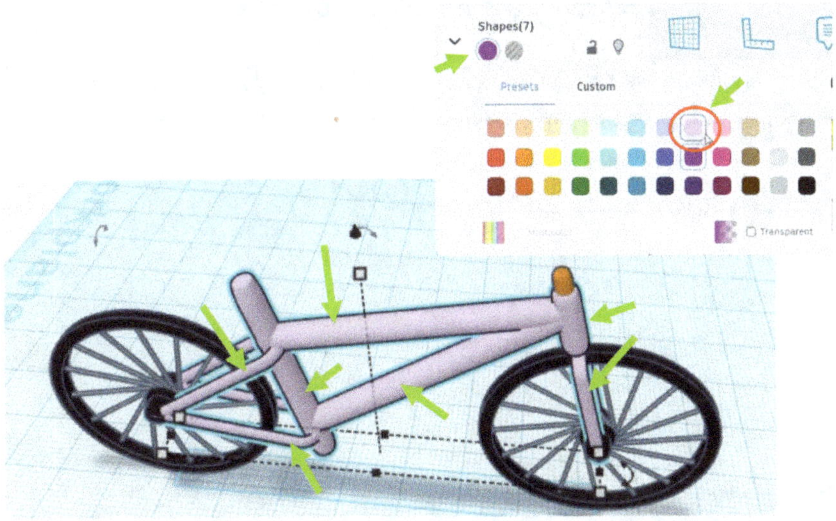

I also changed the color of the part to which we then attach the handlebars.

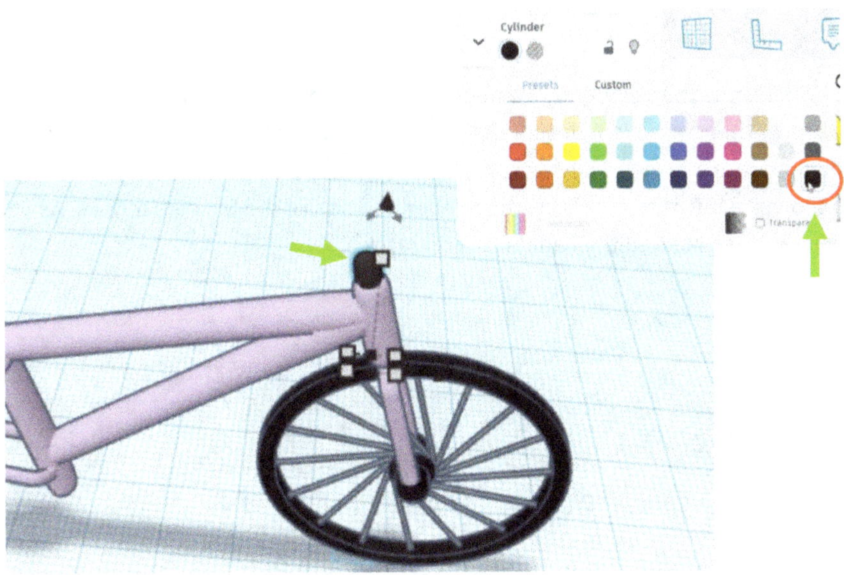

Now we have already come very far, flawlessly done so far! Soon we can complete the project. We are only missing the handlebars, bottom bracket with pedals, and the saddle of the bike. Let's keep going!

3.5 Create the handlebar of the bike

For the handlebar, we start with a cylindrical element ① whose dimensions ②
(③= 19, W= 1.81, H= 1.81) and shape (③ and ④) are modified as shown.

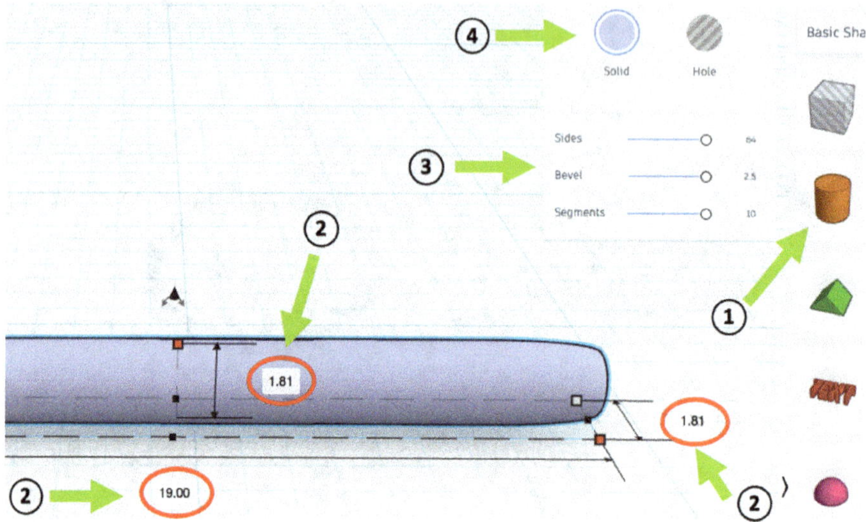

For the rest of the geometry, we duplicate the object we just created, move it up
a bit and change the length to 9 mm ①. Then we move it slightly to the left ②
and duplicate it again ③. After rotating it by 45° ③, we position all three objects
as shown ④. This results in our handlebar and one of the handlebar grips. As you
can see, I also colored the handlebar grip black.

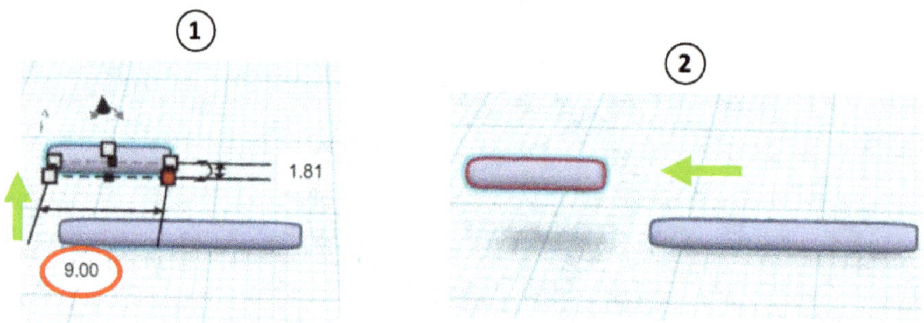

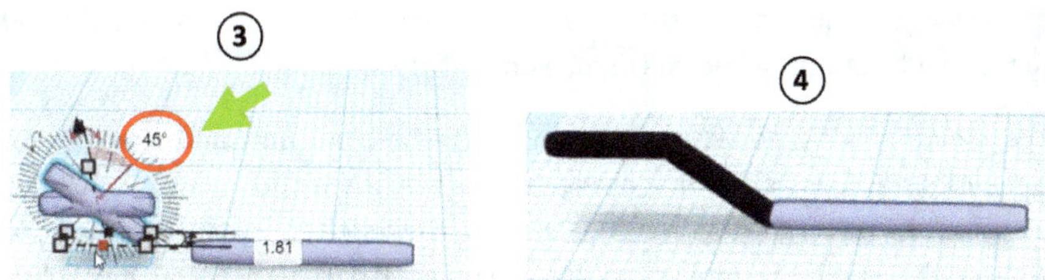

To get a handle on the other side of the handlebar as well, we could now do the same procedure again. However, it is much faster if we first duplicate the handle part ① and then mirror it with the "Mirror" command (② and ③).

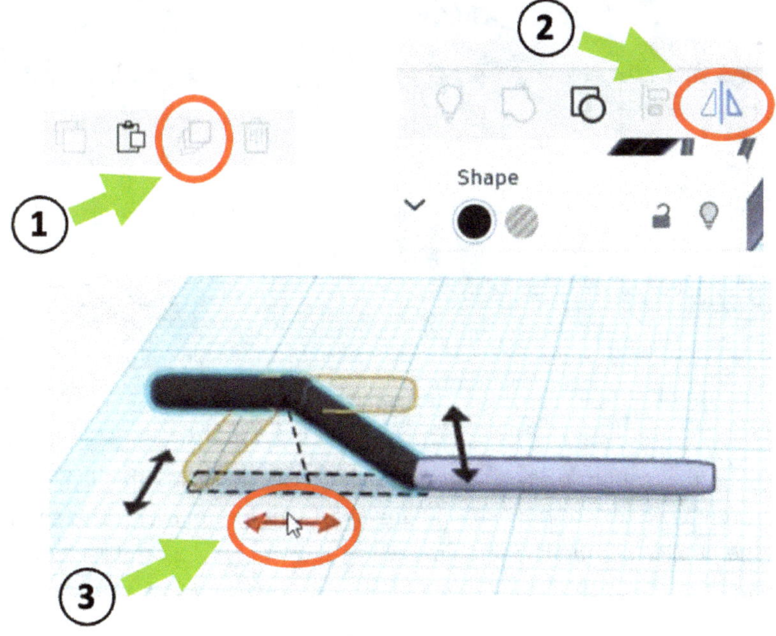

Subsequently, we simply move the duplicated and mirrored handle to the other side.

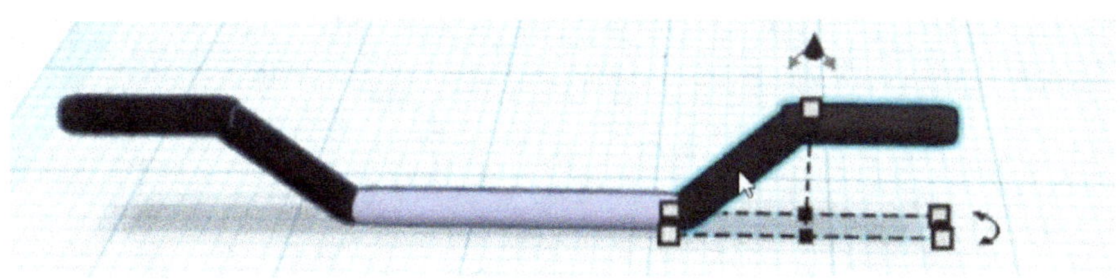

In order to be able to attach the handlebars to the bike later, we now need a body in the middle of the handlebars in the penultimate step.

We create this by duplicating the middle (light blue) part and changing the dimensions as follows. We first change the length of the duplicated part to about 12 mm ①, the height to 2 mm ② and also the width to 2 mm ③. Finally, we shorten the length to 5 mm ④ so that the object is roughly centered and color it black ⑤.

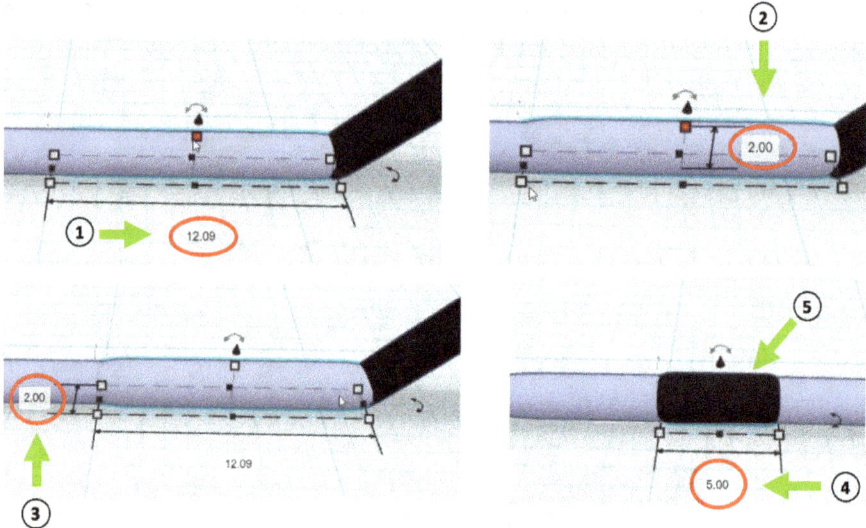

To complete the center part of the handlebar, we duplicate the light blue handlebar rod again, rotate it by 90° ① and shorten it to 4 mm ②. This should position the duplicated object approximately as shown ③. We can then color it black as well.

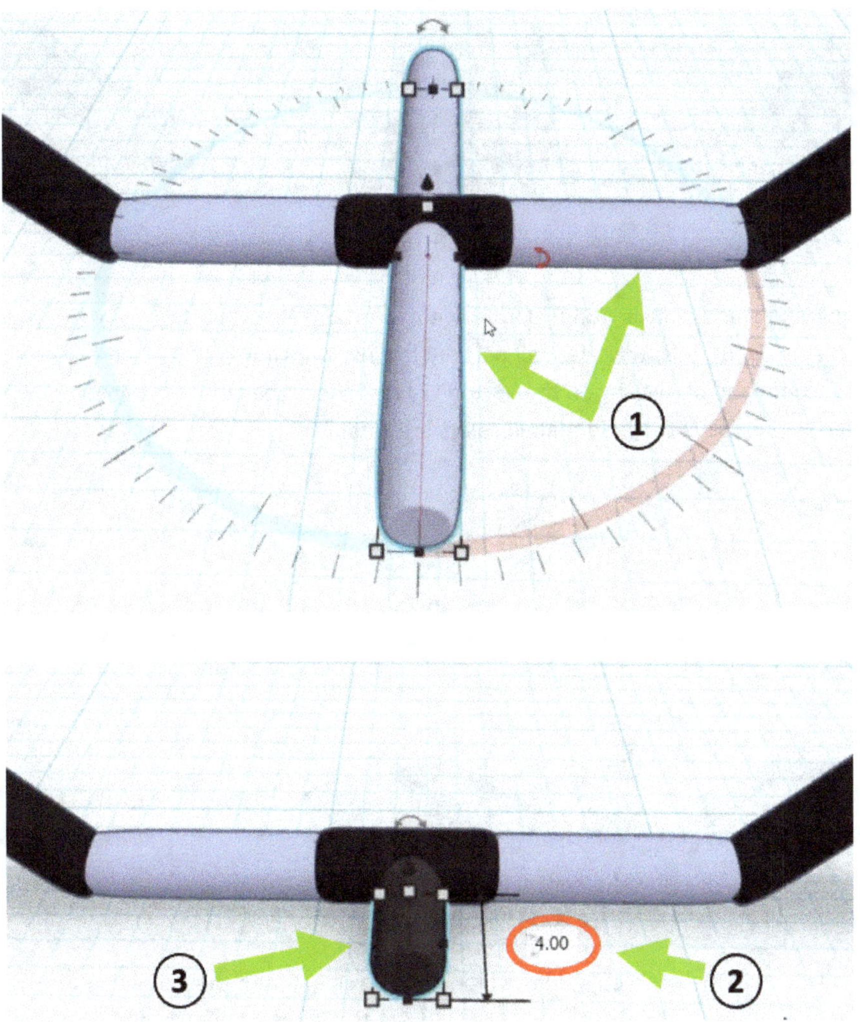

To ensure that the middle black part is concentric with the handlebar (light blue), we select the two parts ("Shift key" pressed) ① and press the "L" key for the "Align" command. We then click successively on the light blue handlebar rod ② and on the alignment points shown in steps ③ and ④.

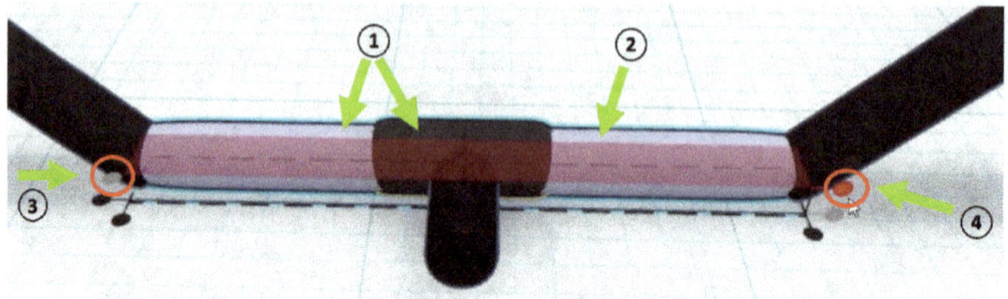

Now our handlebar is done! Before we can mount it on the bike, we group all objects. To do this, we select all parts ①, press the shortcut "CTRL+G" or select the command by clicking on the button ② and check the option "Multicolor" (③ and ④) in the settings so that all colors are retained.

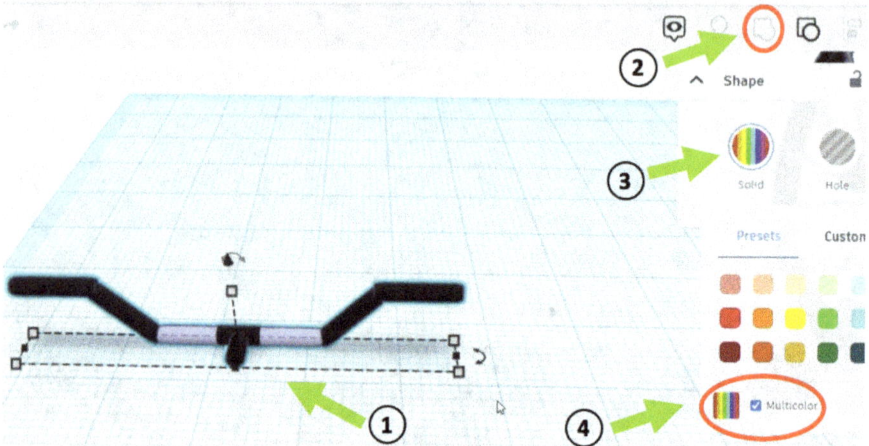

To assemble the handlebar, in the first step, we select both the handlebar ① and the black part of the front fork ② and press the shortcut "L" (for the command "Align"). Then, in the second step, we click again on the black part of the front fork ③ to display the correct alignment points.

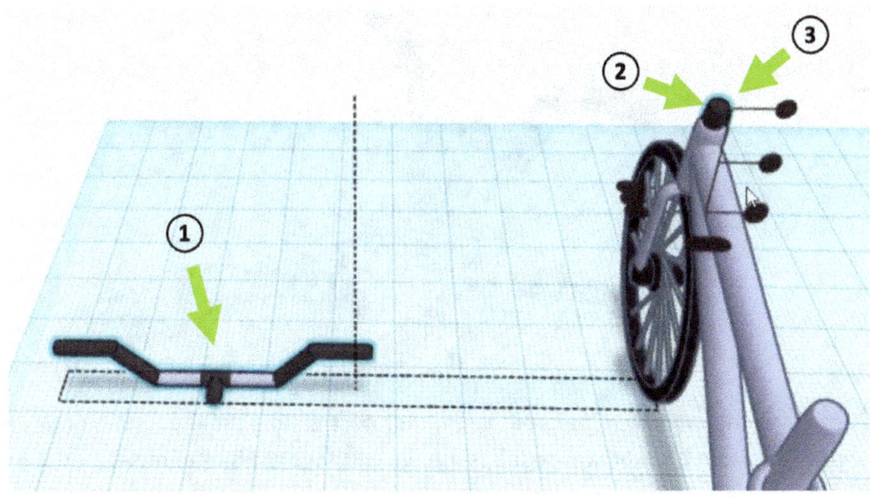

Only then we click on the alignment points shown one after the other so that the handlebars are placed centrally in the front area of the bike.

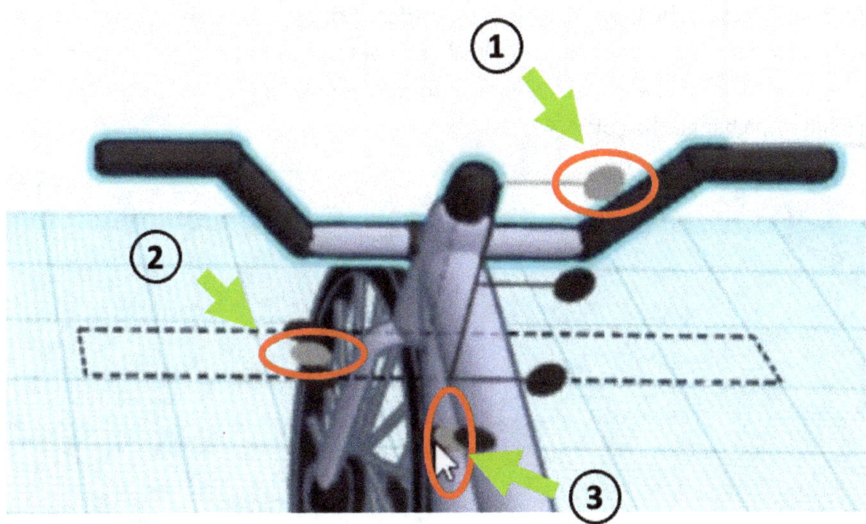

Finally, we need to move the handlebars up a bit.

Perfectly done! We have completed another part of this project. Let's continue with the bottom bracket and pedals, soon we will have the bike completely done!

3.6 The bottom bracket and the pedals of the bicycle

In this chapter, we create the bottom bracket and the pedals of the bike. For the bottom bracket shell, we create a cylindrical body ① whose height and side lengths should be 7.25 mm each ②. We also set the settings "Sides", "Bevel" and "Segments" ③ to the respective maximum values (64, 2.5, 10), as is often the case. Finally, we change the color ④.

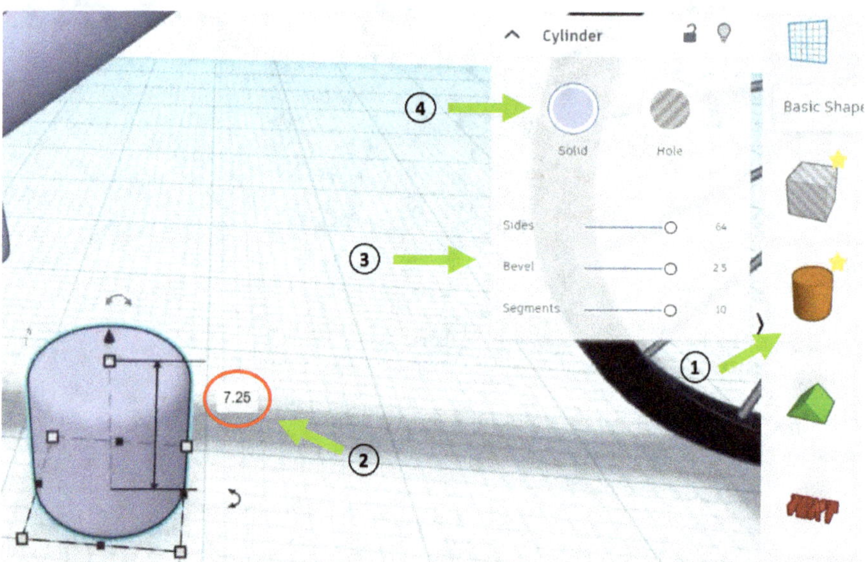

We then rotate this object by 90° and position it centrally in the lower area of the bicycle frame (move the object and use the command "Align").

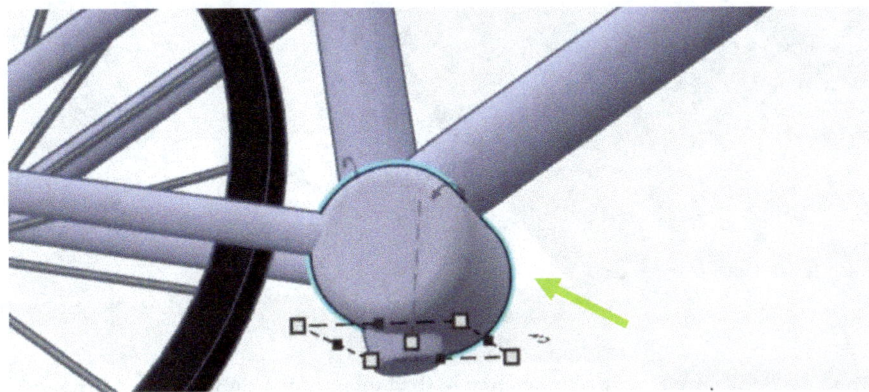

It is noticeable that the bicycle frame still protrudes somewhat in the lower area. We would now like to remove this protrusion. How could we do that? First try it yourself, the solution follows immediately.

-- Solution follows here--

We place our work plane on the lower surface of the overhanging part using the shortcut "W" and then we can easily shorten it by dragging the overhang upwards with the mouse.

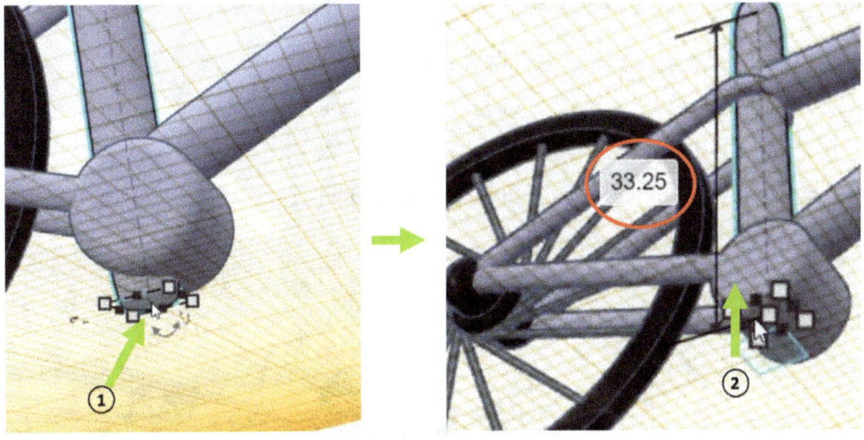

Now we continue with the bottom bracket and pedals, which we will then position in the bottom bracket shell.

We first create the bottom bracket from a black colored cylindrical object. The dimensions are: Width = 4mm, Height = 4 mm and Length = 9 mm.

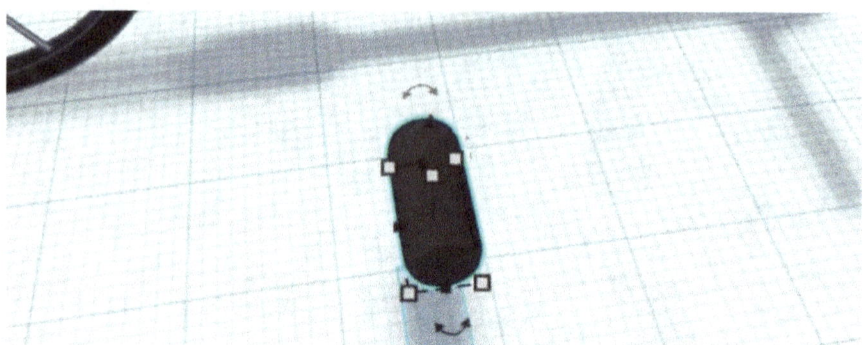

Then we duplicate this object and change the length of the duplicate to 11 mm and its height and width to 1.81 mm each.

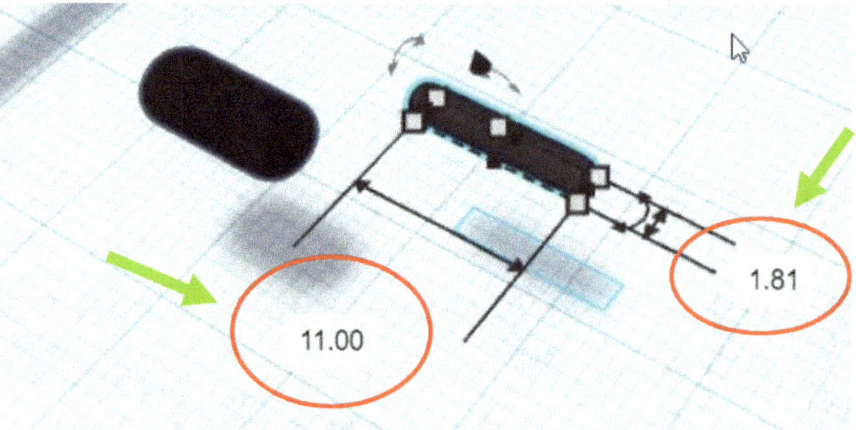

We duplicate and move this part twice so that we get the object shown, which is our pedal crank.

After a rotation, we can connect this pedal crank centered with the bottom bracket.

Now only the two pedals are missing. We create the pedals from a cube geometry ("Dice"). We can find this geometry in the shape library ①. To create our pedal, we change the dimensions of the cube to 10 mm for the length, 4 mm for the width and 2 mm for the height ②.

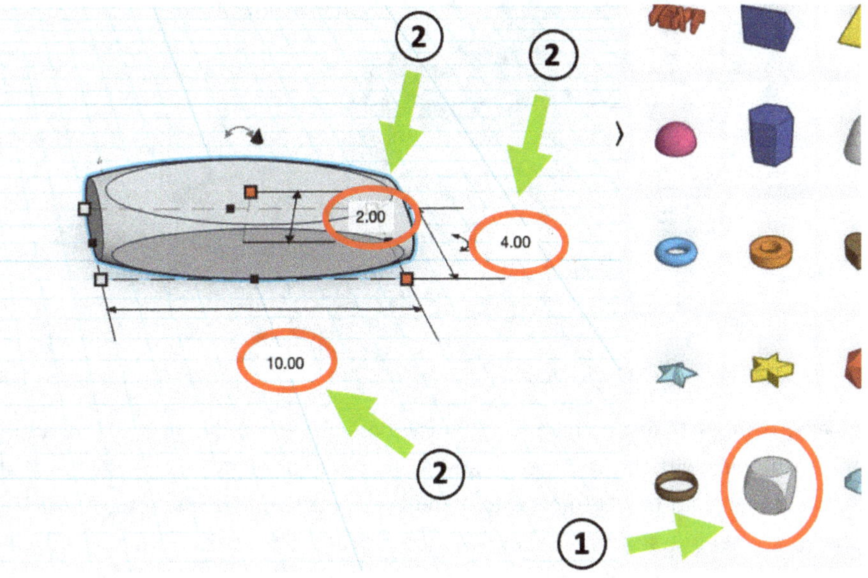

After a rotation and shift, we can position the first pedal.

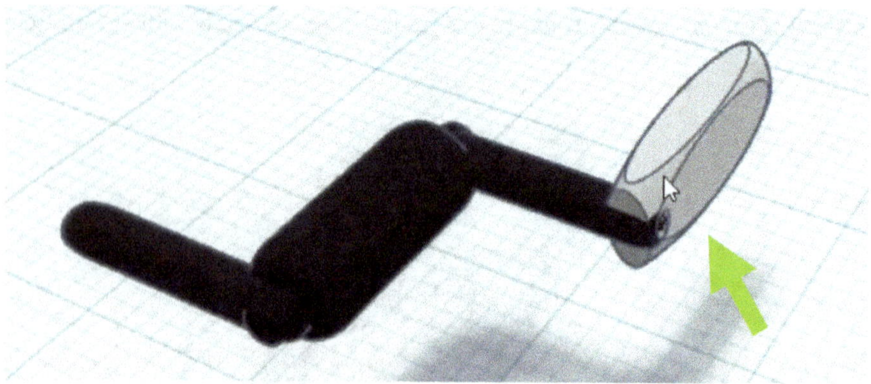

Then we duplicate the first pedal and move it to the other side to get the second pedal. In addition, we group the composite of bottom bracket, crank, and pedals by selecting all the parts and using the shortcut "CTRL+G". Remember to activate the option "Multicolor" to keep the different colors.

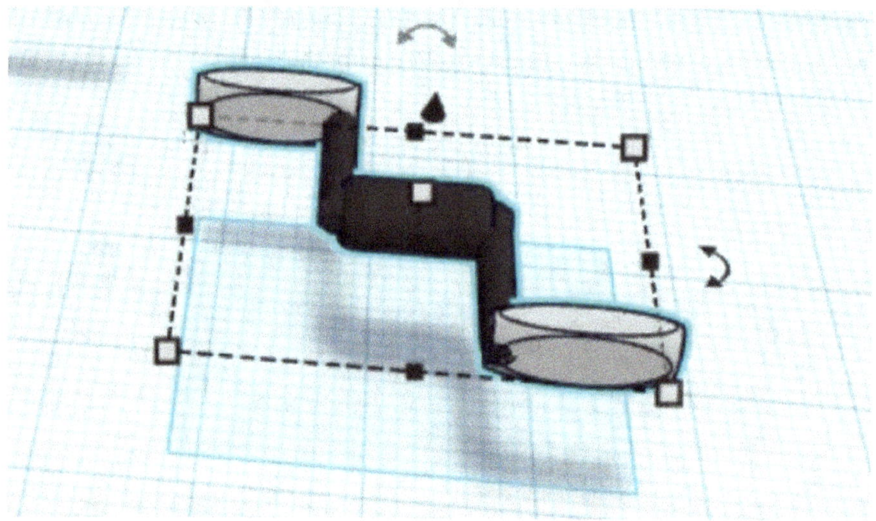

Finally, we need to install the bottom bracket assembly into the bike. We carry out the positioning with the short command "L" (command "Align"). To do this, we first select the bottom bracket group ① (Shift key pressed) and the bottom bracket shell ②. After pressing the "L" key, we then click again on the bottom bracket shell ③ so that the correct alignment points appear. Now we select each of the middle alignment points ④.

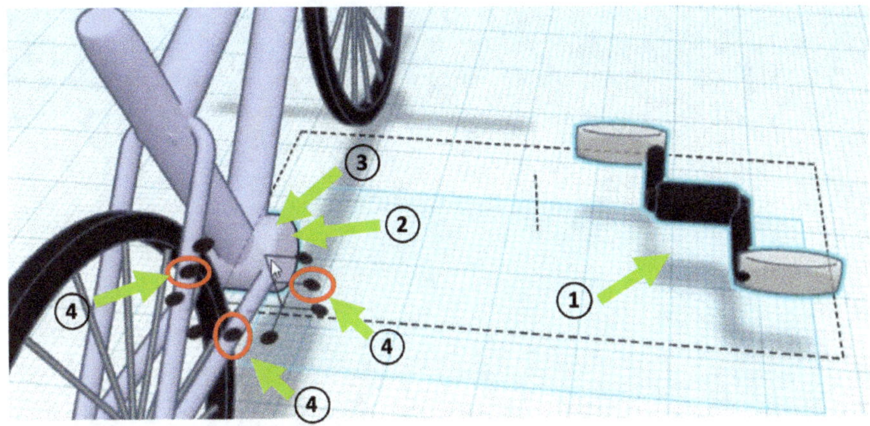

Only the saddle for the bike is missing, then we have the project done! Stay tuned, almost done!

3.7 The saddle of the bicycle

We create the bicycle saddle with the basic object "Paraboloid" ① from the shape library. After we have rotated the object ② by 90°, we need to perform a few more steps.

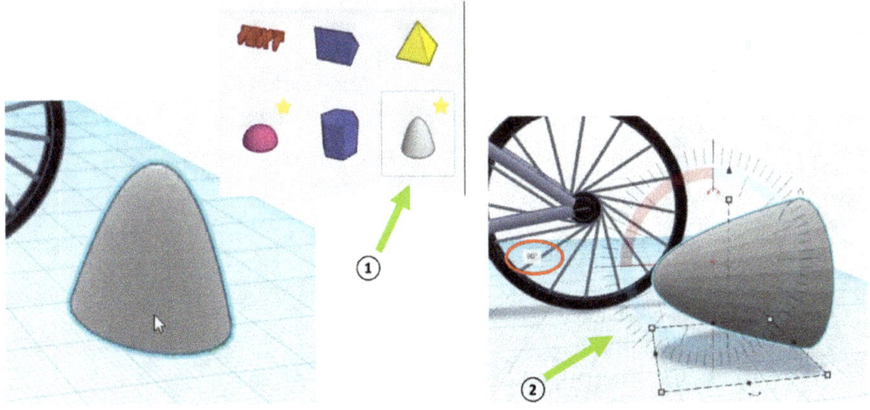

First, we change the height of the rotated object to 7 mm ① and second, we duplicate the part and drag the duplicate ② backwards with the mouse in the direction of the orange arrow ③. Then we change the width of both objects to 15 mm ④.

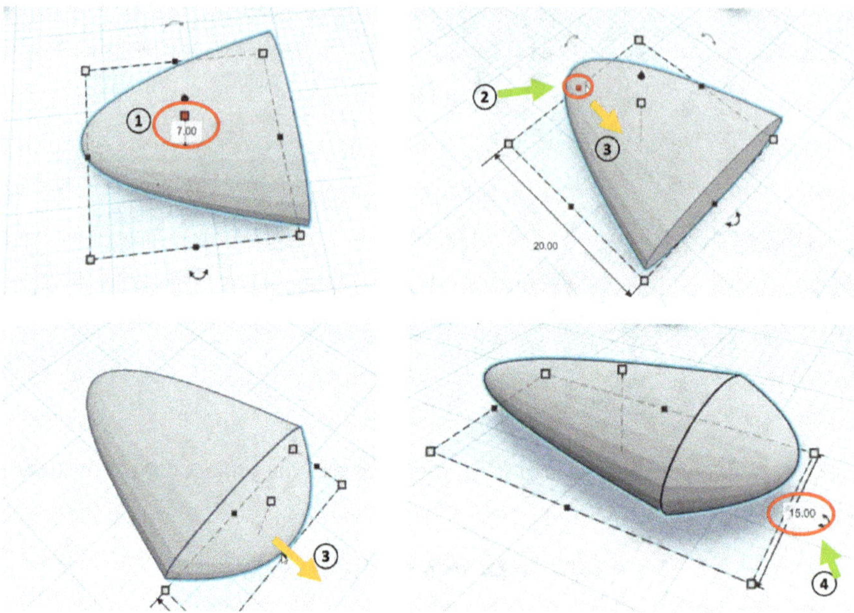

Afterward, we duplicate the part and remove the bottom of the saddle by setting the duplicated object to "Hole", moving it down 1 mm and then grouping both objects together ("CTRL+G").

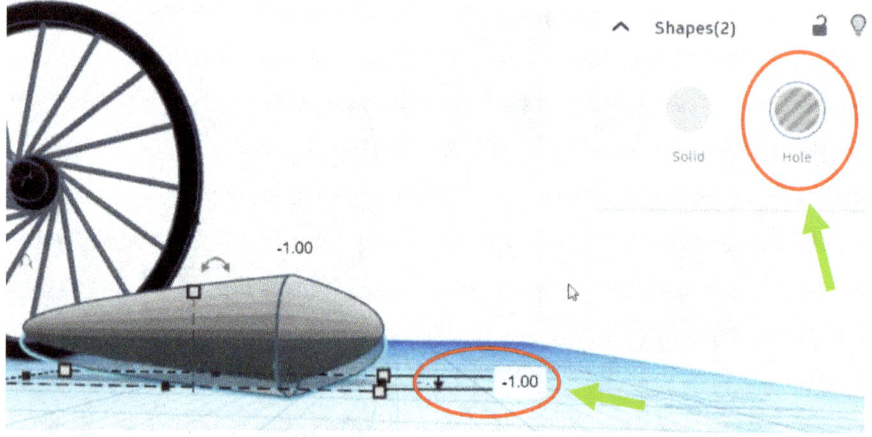

The saddle turned out a bit too big in my opinion, so I changed the dimensions of the grouped object a bit again. I shortened the length to 20 mm and the width to 12 mm. The height remains at 4 mm.

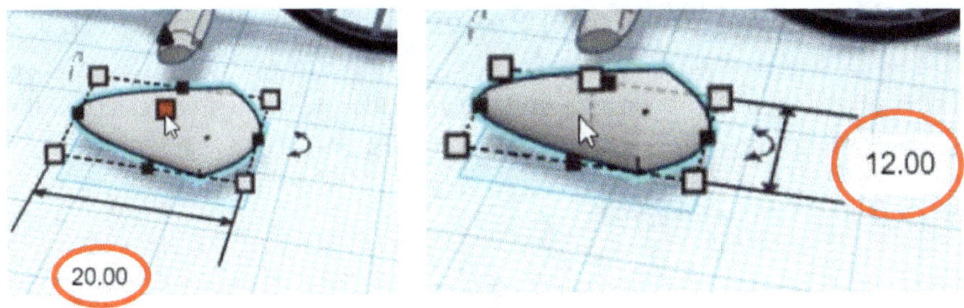

Finally, we can color the saddle as desired, e.g., in black, and then move and position it using your mouse. For the central alignment, you can use the command "Align".

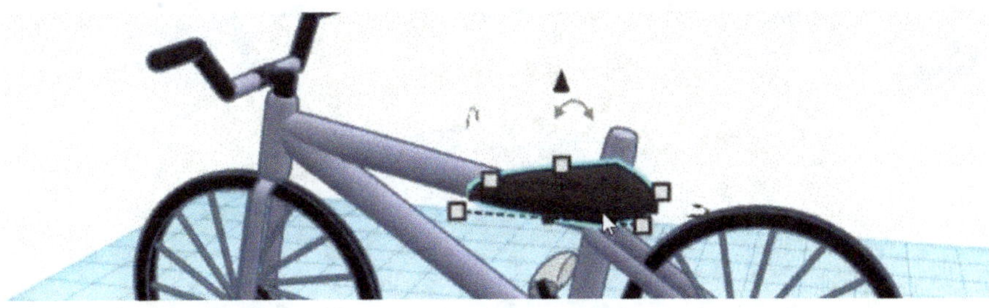

Wow. That was quite a long and complex project. If you got this far, you can be very proud of yourself. You've done quite a bit with it and practiced a lot in "Tinkercad". The finished bike should look something like this. Of course, it's not a big deal if your bike looks a little different or if you've chosen different colors. Be creative and think for yourself, that's just right!

Chapter 4 | 3D Model Project 3: Retro Alarm Clock

In this third project, we will create a retro alarm clock. As always, you can copy the finished model into your "Tinkercad" account using the following link:

https://tinyurl.com/3mererah

In the construction, we proceed as follows. First, we start with the alarm clock case, then we create the clock face and the hands. Then come the bells and the hammer that would make the bells ring. Finally, we add the white on/off switch at the top and the feet at the bottom. All this we do step by step.

74

4.1 The housing of the alarm clock

First of all, the housing of the alarm clock consists of a cylindrical base body, the length, and width of which we increase to 150 mm and the height to 65 mm. We can also assign the yellow color at this step.

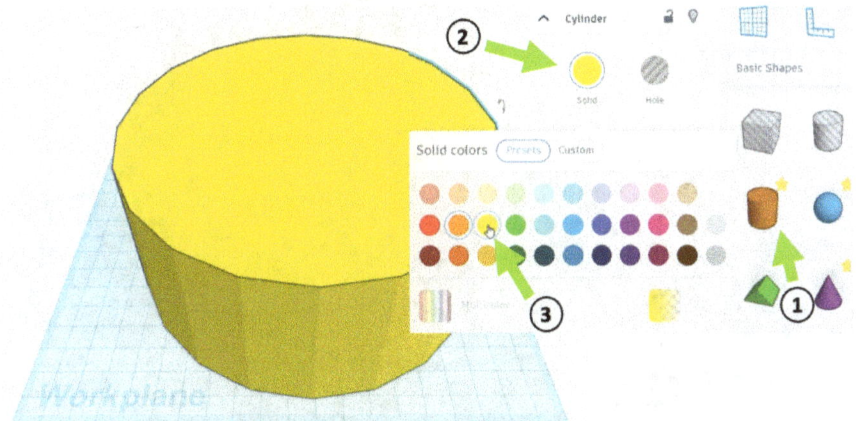

Since the shape is still a bit too angular for me, we increase all parameters in the object's settings to the respective maximum (64, 2.5, 10). To do this, simply drag all three sliders all the way to the right.

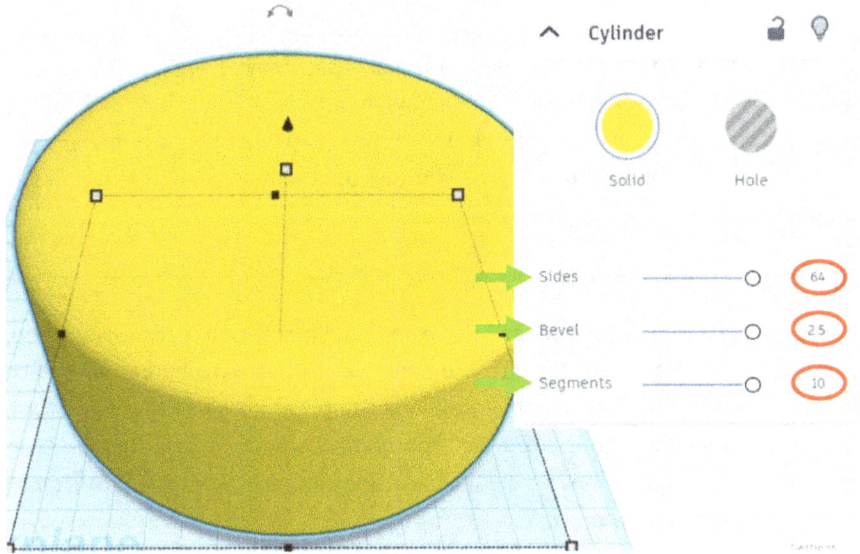

Now we want to make room for the dial and the hands. For this purpose, our previous cylinder should take the following shape:

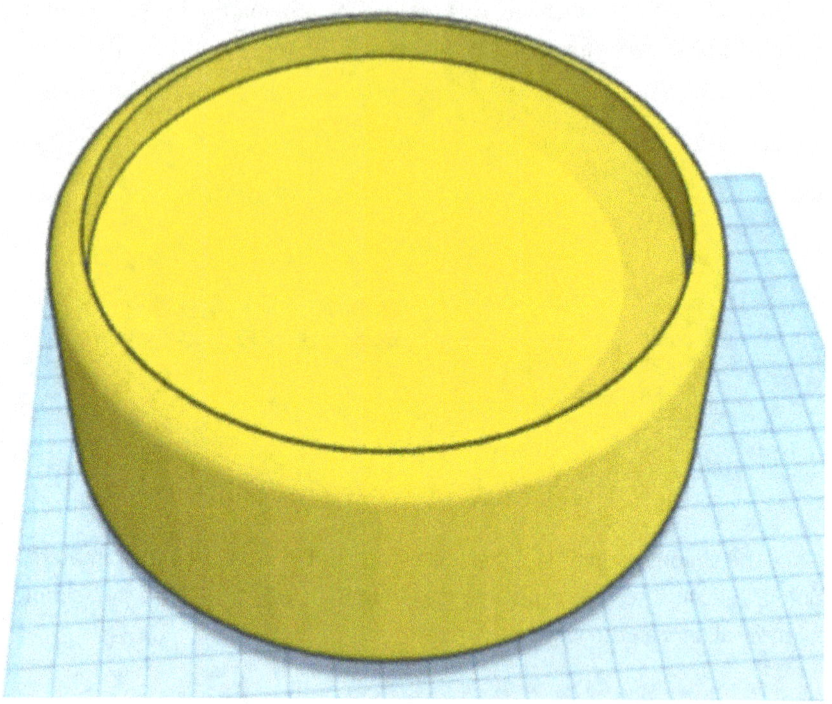

Feel free to think about how we might approach this. Maybe you'll come up with the solution completely on your own by now. In any case, it won't hurt if you try things out yourself for a while at this point. You can first work by eye and then take the correct measurements later. Otherwise, I would give away too many clues at this point.

-------------------------------------- Solution follows here --------------------------------------

We create the desired geometry by using a body similar to the already existing one, with which we create a section. That means we subtract two bodies with each other. To create the similar body, we simply duplicate the existing clock case (CTRL+D), change the settings to "Hole" and center the two bodies using the Align command ("L"). Then we move the duplicated body up a bit so that it has a distance of 46 mm from the bottom.

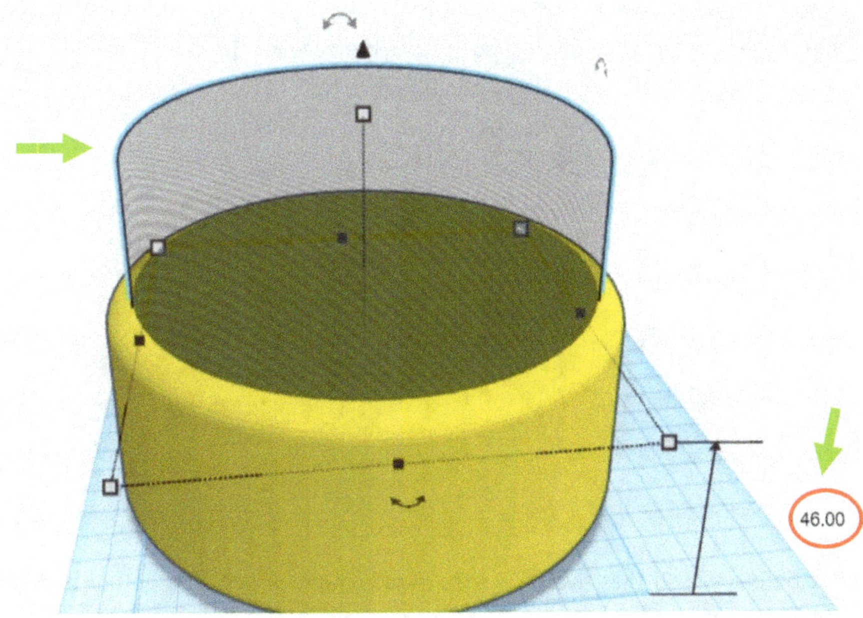

In the next step, we change the settings for the upper body. To make the cutout look as desired, we set the values 64, 2 and 1 for the settings "Sides", "Bevel" and "Segments".

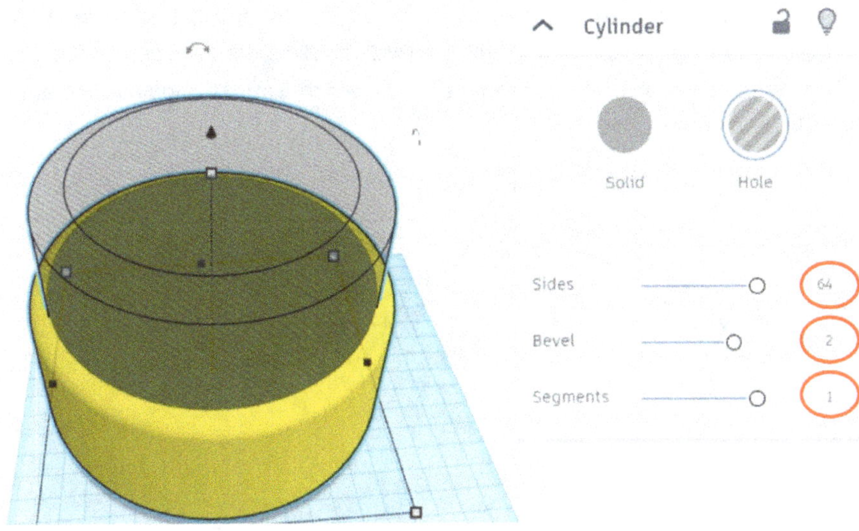

Before we group the two bodies together, we duplicate the upper body ("CTRL+D") and move it to the side. This will be used as the base for the clock face.

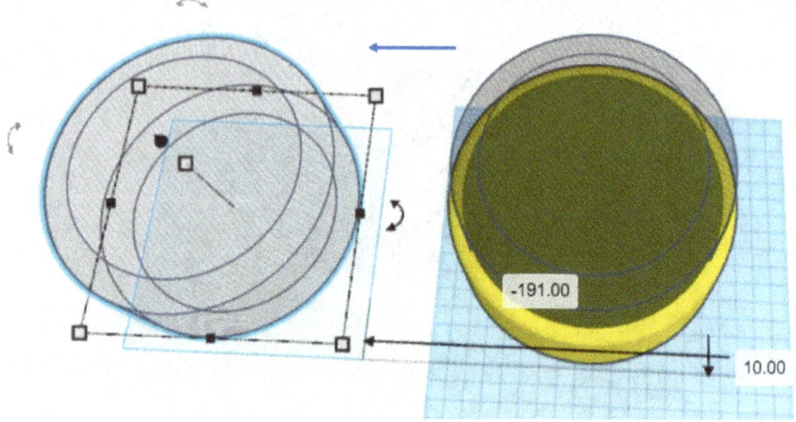

But before we do that, we group the two composite bodies together and thus obtain the desired case.

4.2 The dial and hands of the alarm clock

Next, we'll turn our attention to the clock face. We have already done some preliminary work on this in the previous chapter by duplicating an object and moving it to the side. We will first set this object to the selection "Solid", then change the color to white and reduce the height to 3 mm. It should represent the background of the clock face.

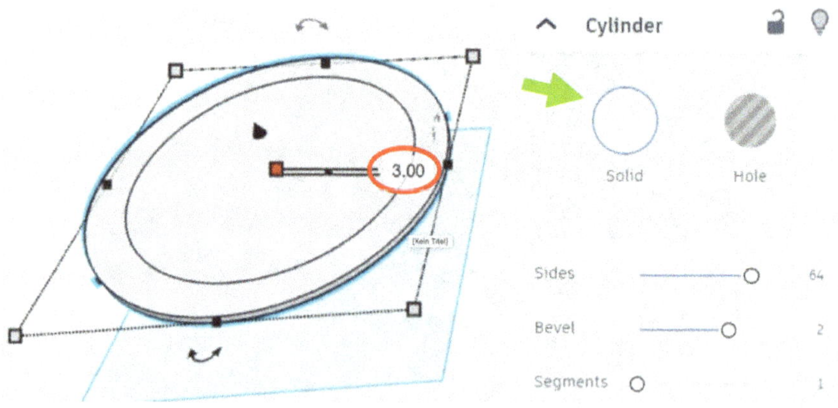

With the Align command (key "L") we center the dial and the case.

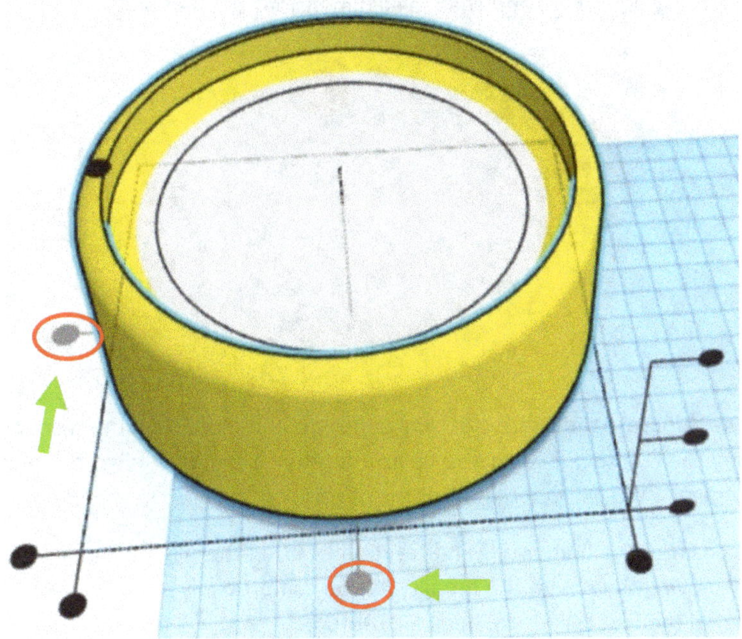

Then we move the dial to a distance of approx. 51 mm from the working plane.

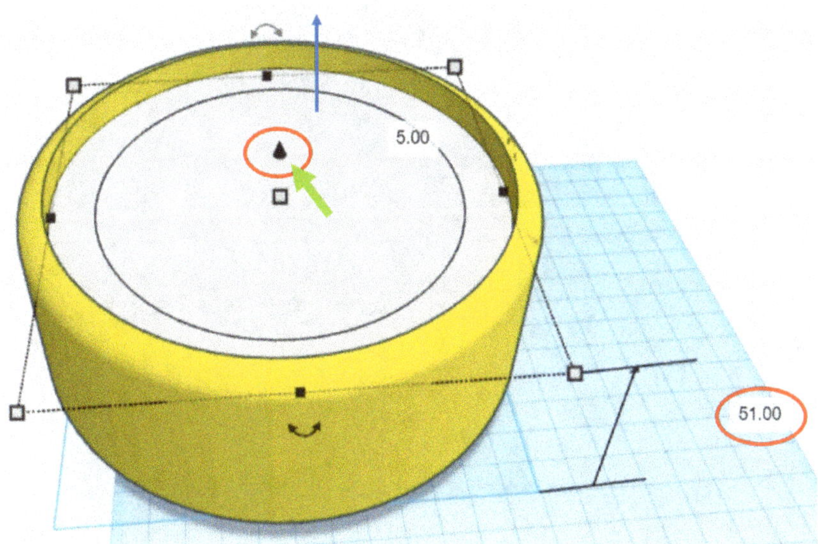

We then create the other elements for the clock face. We again use a cylindrical basic shape ①, increase its parameters ("Sides", "Bevel", "Segments") to their respective maximum ② and change all dimensions to 14 mm ③.

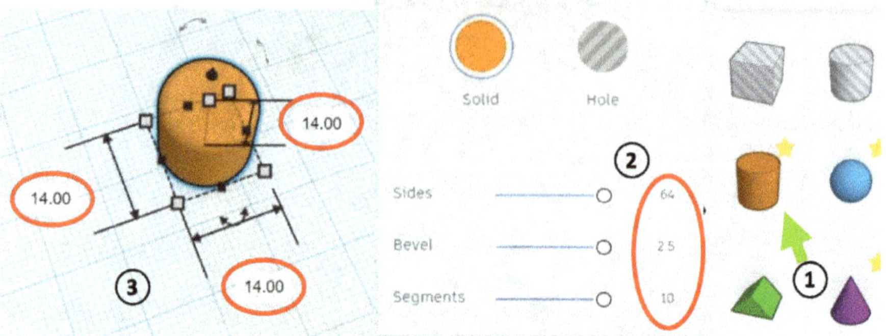

Then we duplicate the white clock face, move it and place it on the work plane by pressing the "D" key. It will serve us as a reference to better align the bodies for the numerals. We will delete it after the alignment.

Let us position the first two cylindrical bodies using the Align command (key "L") and by moving them with the mouse. As you can probably already guess, I simply duplicated the first cylindrical body ("CTRL+D").

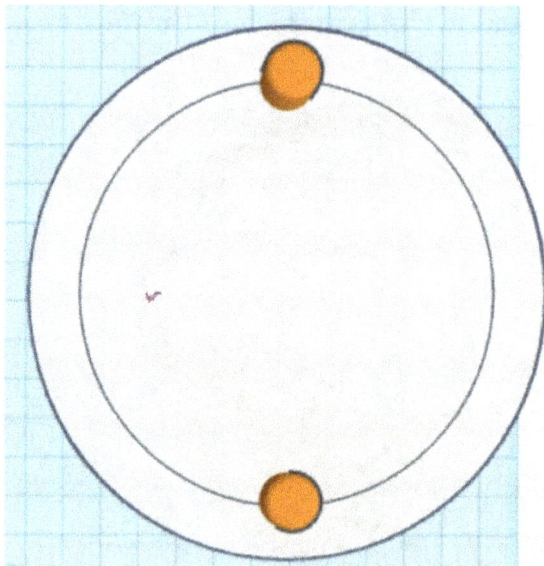

Then we group these two cylindrical bodies with the command "Group" ("CTRL+G") so that we can create a pattern afterward. I also changed the color to red. If we now duplicate the grouped bodies with "CTRL+D" and then rotate them by 30° with the computer mouse, we get the first part of the pattern.

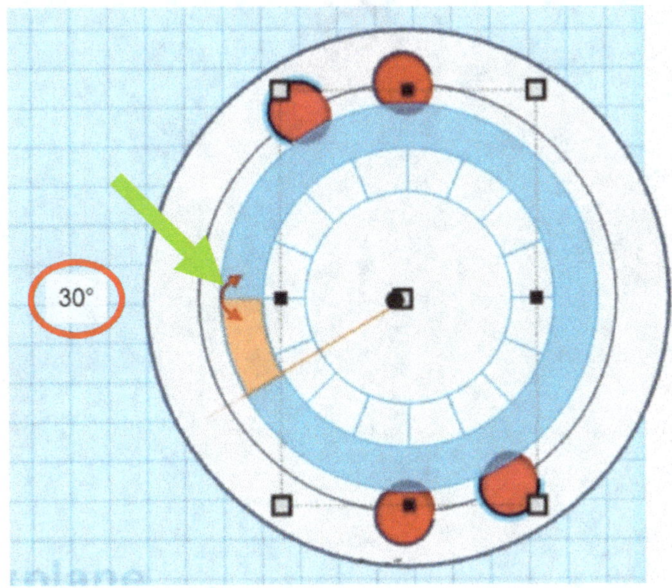

We then do it four more times, obtaining a total of twelve cylindrical bodies.

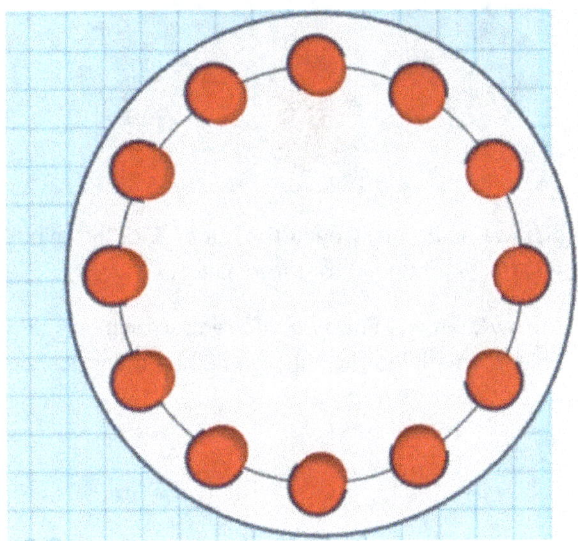

Thereafter, I change the color of some dials and delete the duplicated clock face, which – as I said – served as a reference only. Finally, we have to group the objects together (activate the option "Multicolor").

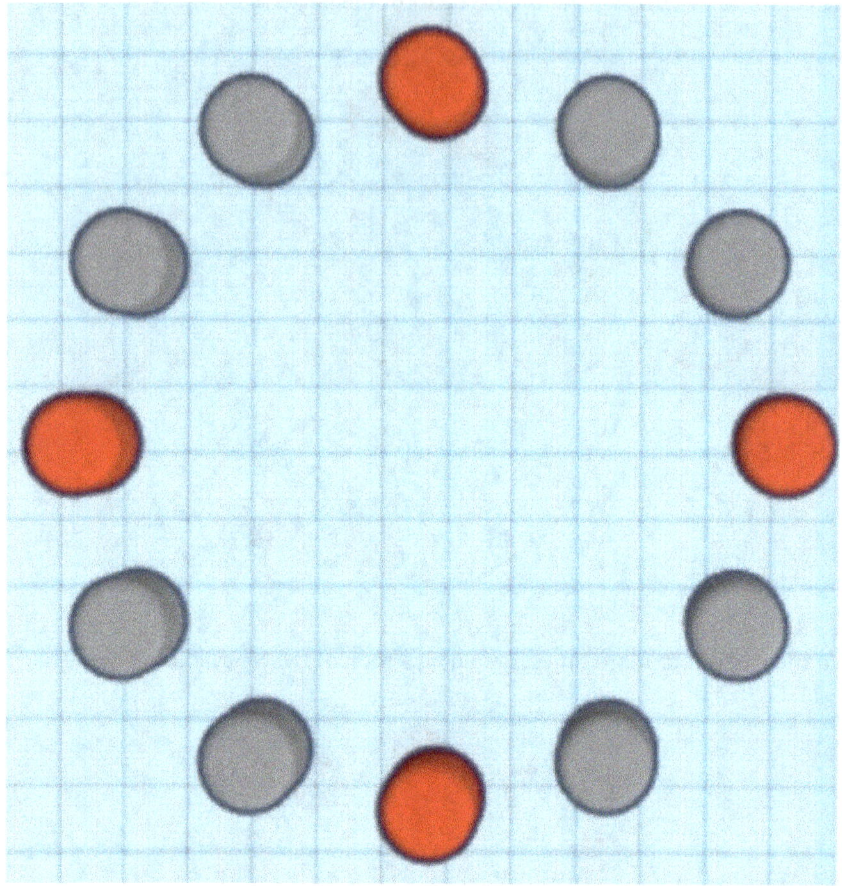

To complete the dial, we additionally need the hour hand, the minute hand, the second hand and an attachment point for these hands.

By searching for "Arrow", we will find two different arrowheads and put one of each on our work plane. In addition to this, we need a cylindrical object for the body of the hands.

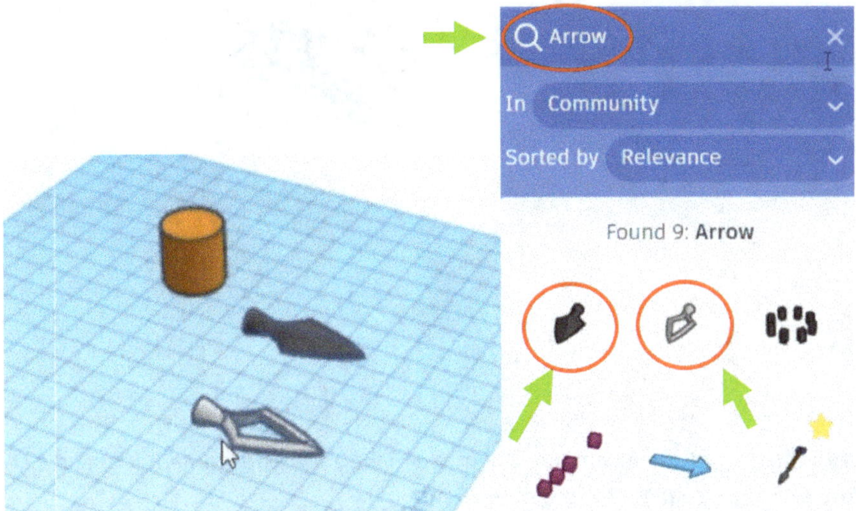

We change the dimensions of the cylindrical body to 7 mm each for length and width, leaving the height at the default value for now. Then we set the parameter "Sides" to the value 64 and duplicate and rotate the cylindrical body so that we get the following result.

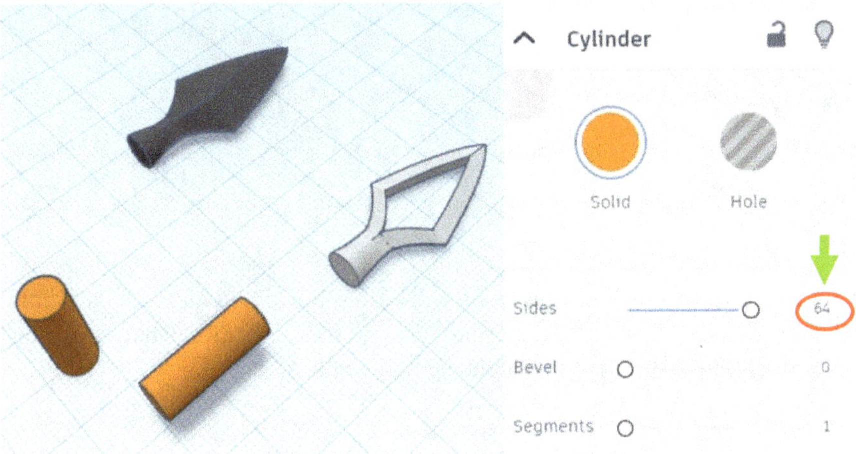

Now we can use the command "Workplane tool" to place the cylindrical body on the pointer tip. You can press the "W" key as a shortcut, then select the plane ① of the pointer tip, select the cylindrical body ② and finally press the "D" key to do the positioning.

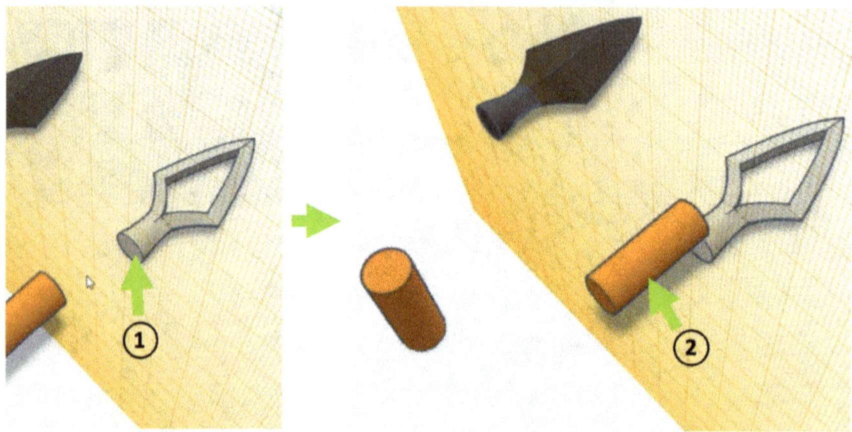

With the help of the command "Align" we make another alignment (①　and ②).
Afterward, we change the length to 26 mm ③.

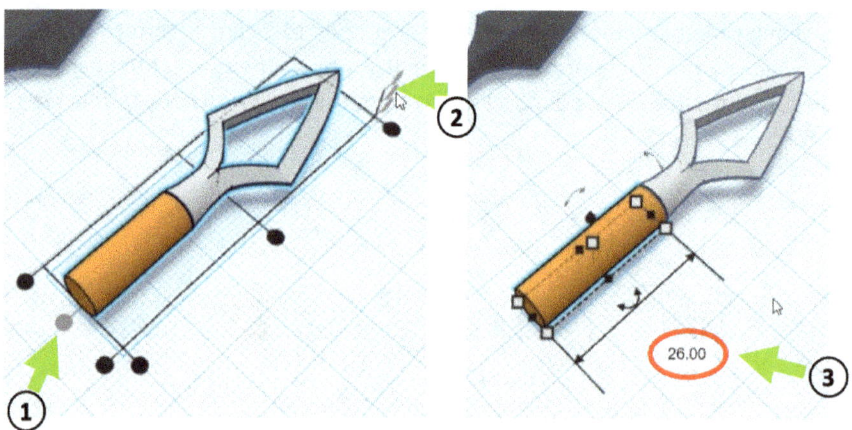

Now we have to do the same steps with the other pointer tip and the other
cylindrical body. Next, we color the two cylindrical bodies white and gray,
respectively, so that we get two monochrome pointers.

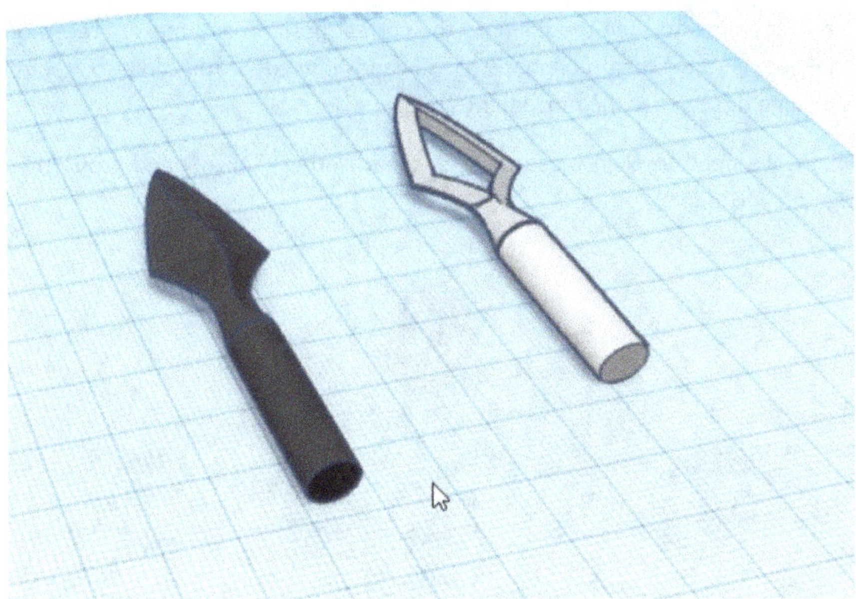

In the next step, we take care of the mounting point of the hands, more precisely, the hub of the movement. Again, we use a cylindrical body whose dimensions (length, width, height) we change to 10 mm each. Then we use the commands "Duplicate and repeat" as well as "Mirror", "Group" and "Align" to position the hands as shown at the hub of the movement. You can also play with the length and size of the hands by dragging them with the mouse. In the end, just you have to like it!

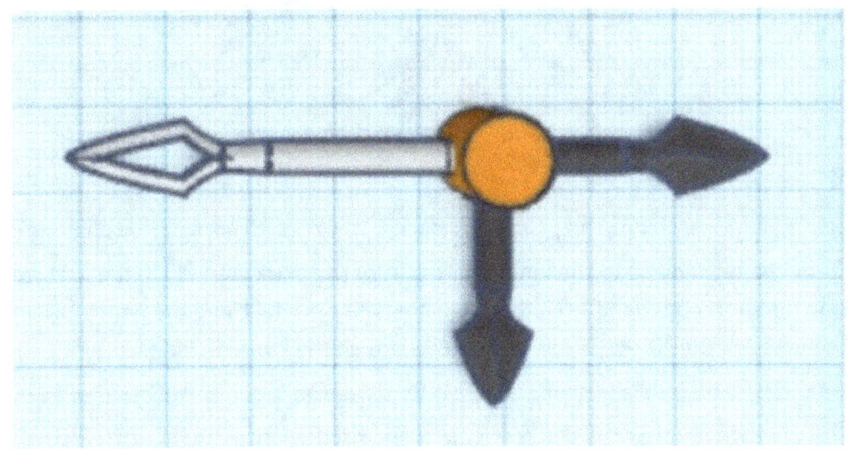

The next step is to slide the dial into the correct position and make a few more adjustments to the length or shape of the hands if needed. You can also feel free to change the color of the movement's hub.

Finally, we need to align these objects to each other ("Align") and group them together ("Group").

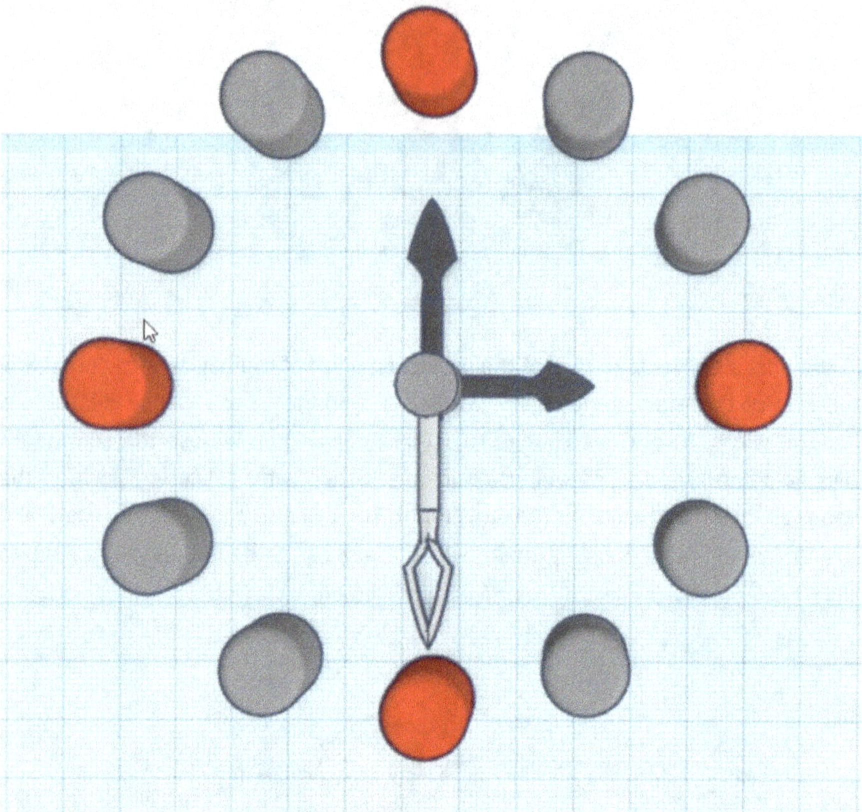

After that, we mount the dial including the hands in the watch case. We do this by setting the work plane to the inner white part of the clock case ① in the first step using the short command "W", then selecting the clock face and the hands ② and then pressing the "D" key. Now the objects are on the correct plane.

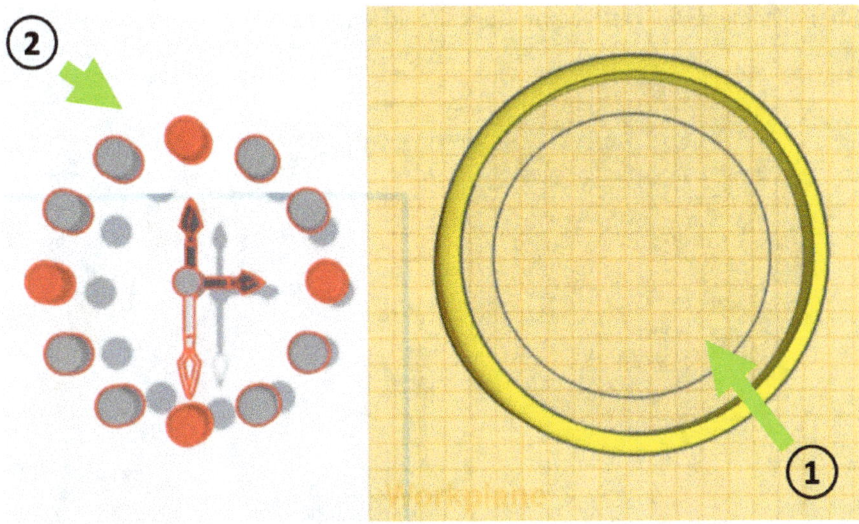

Before we use the "Align" command for further alignment as usual, we first duplicate the white background of the clock face ① and move the duplicate ② upwards. We will need it later as the front panel.

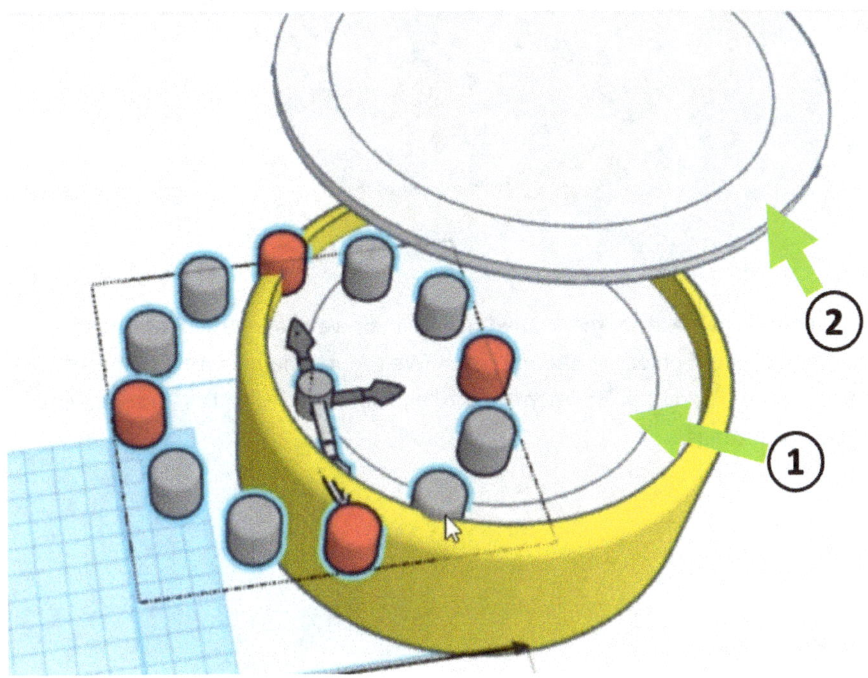

After alignment, our retro alarm clock should look like this:

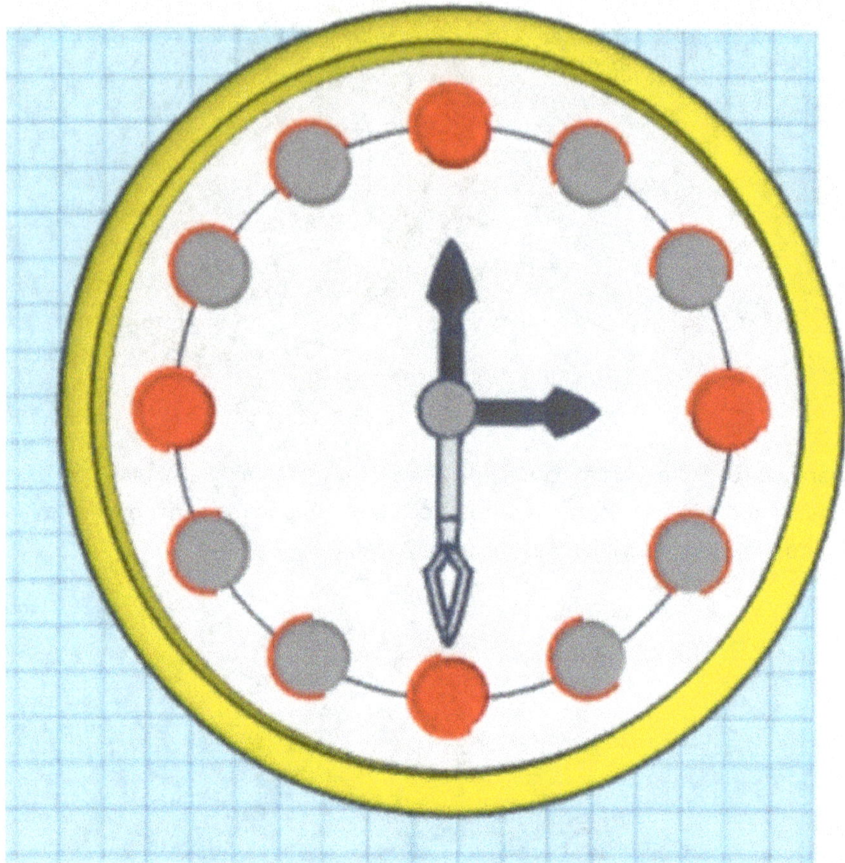

To create the previously mentioned front panel, we change the length and width of the duplicated object to 140 mm each. We reduce the height to 1 mm. We also increase the parameter "Segments" to 10 and activate the option "Transparent" in the color settings.

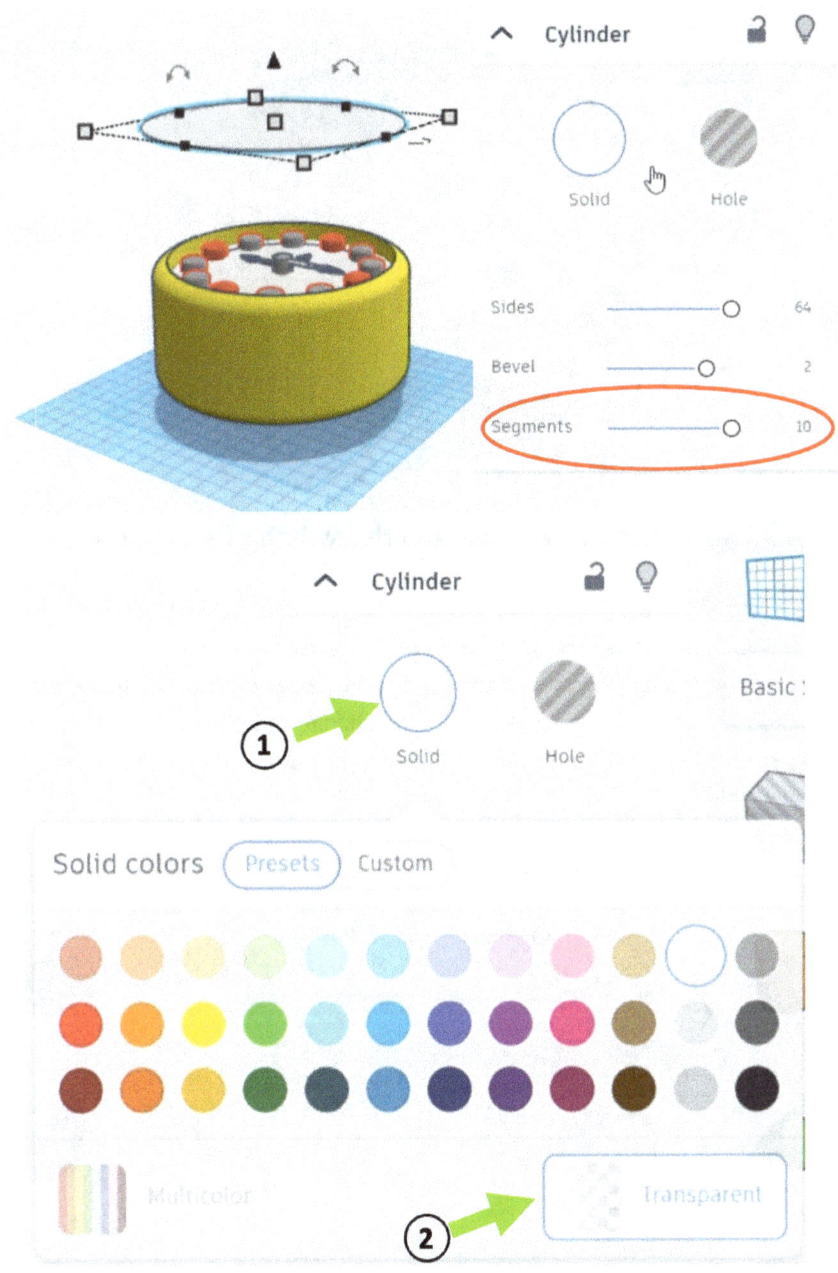

Then we center the slice with the command "Align" and move it down a bit to the correct position.

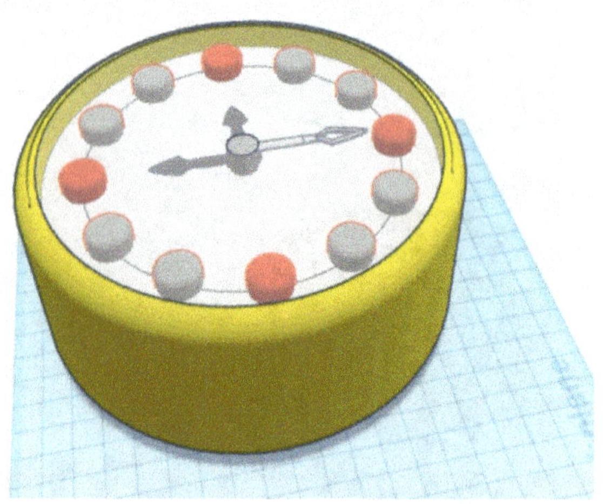

4.3 The bells, the hammer, and the switch of the alarm clock

Excellent! After we have grouped all the previous objects (select option: "Multicolor"), we take care of the bells of the retro alarm clock. As a basic body, we use a hemisphere ①, which we can find in the shape library. Thereafter, you can choose a color (for example, gray) and change the dimensions. We need 68 mm each for the length and width (② and ③) and 17 mm for the height ④ of the hemisphere.

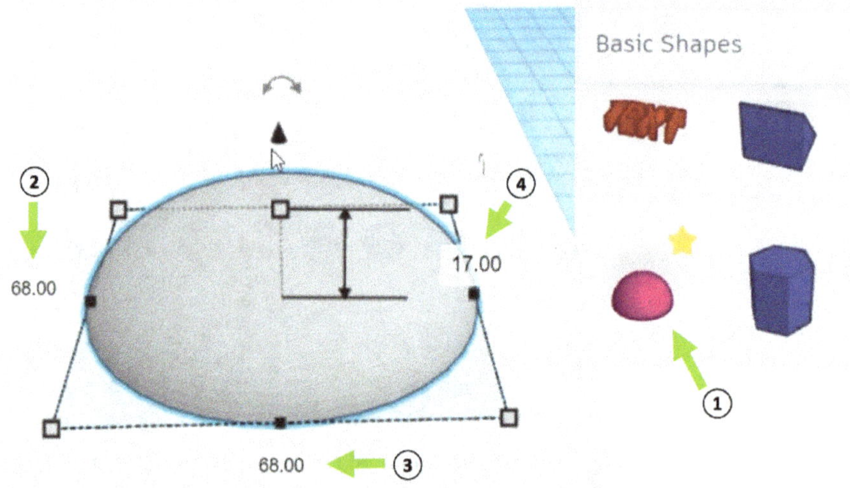

To hollow out the solid hemisphere, we use a simple trick. We duplicate the hemisphere, move the duplicate 3 mm upwards ② and change the setting of the source object to "Hole" (③ and ④). After that, we group the two objects and thus get a hollowed hemisphere.

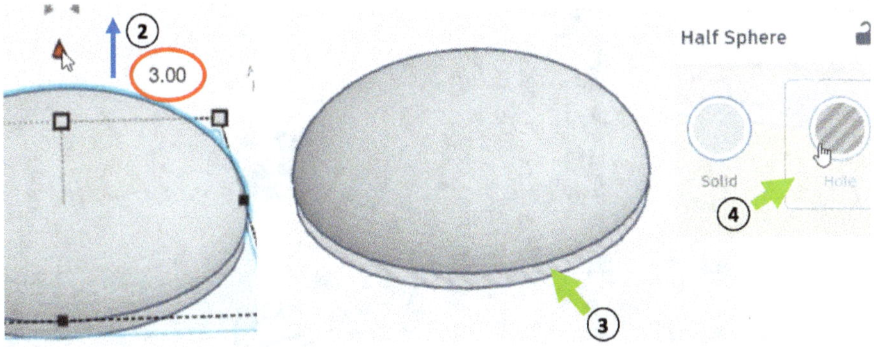

To be able to mount this bell on the retro alarm clock, we need a suspension, which we create from a cylindrical body ① and a paraboloid ② in the next step.

The dimensions for the <u>cylindrical body</u> are 5 mm each for the length and width and 70 mm for the height. We leave the height of the <u>paraboloid</u> at the preset 20 mm but change the length and width to 5 mm each.

To position the two parts on top of each other, we use the command "Workplane tool" on the one hand and the commands "Align" and "Group" on the other hand. You can probably do this on your own by now. The suspension should then look like this.

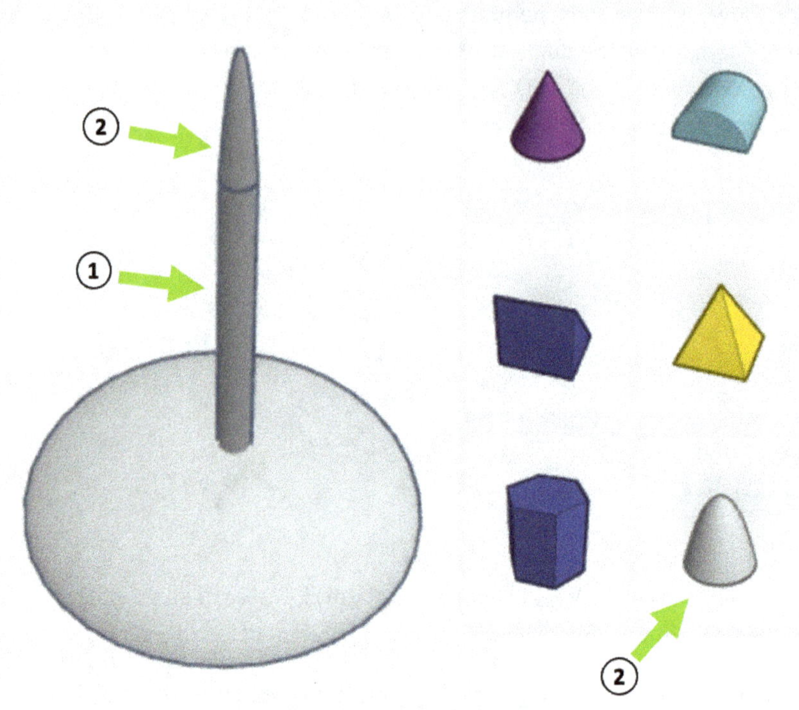

Now we need to move the bell up a bit, you can approximate the position by eye.

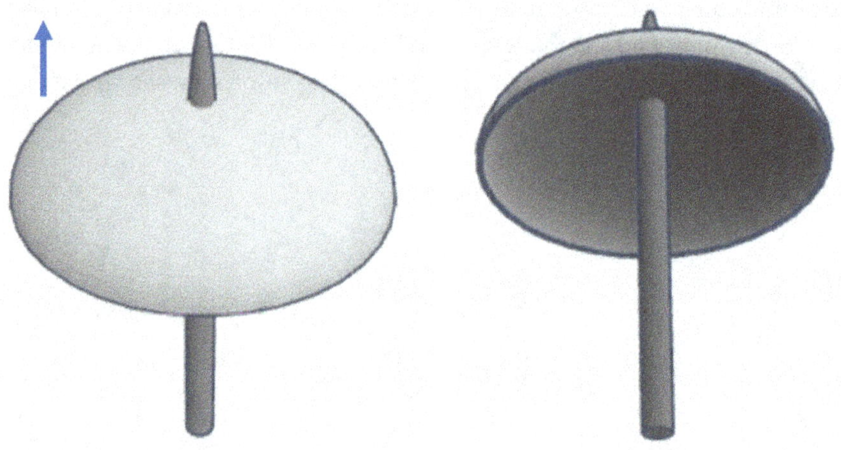

Then we rotate (22.5°) and duplicate the bell including the suspension, since we need two of them in total. We also use the command "Mirror" so that the duplicated objects are positioned opposite rotated.

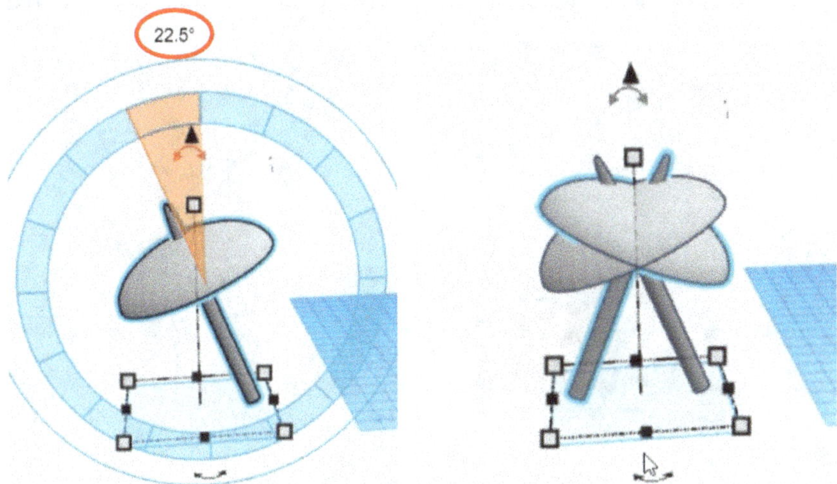

Now we need to move the duplicated objects a bit to the side. We also need to rotate the alarm clock so that it is upright. Afterward, we can move the two bells to the top of the alarm clock and center them with the "Align" command.

Now we create the hammer of the alarm clock. We will assemble it from two basic cylindrical bodies. One of them should be 5 mm wide and long and 60 mm high ①, the other one 15 mm wide and long and 20 mm high ②. We turn the thicker body by 90 degrees and position it on the long narrow body. We also change the colors.

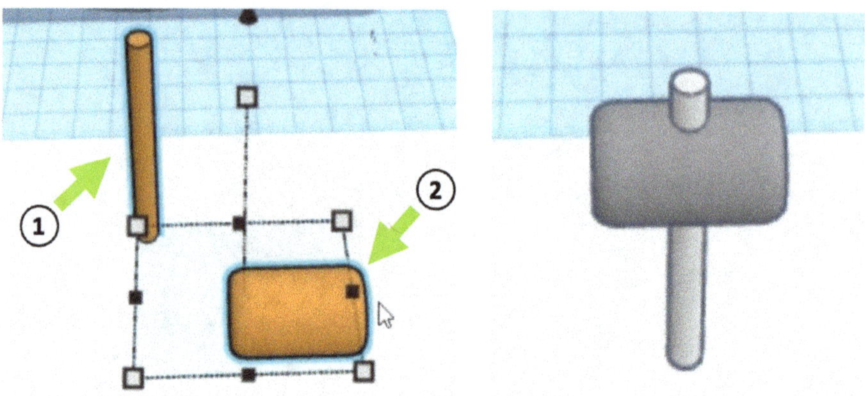

You can then group the hammer (option: "Multicolor" activated in the color settings) and position it between the bells of the alarm clock.

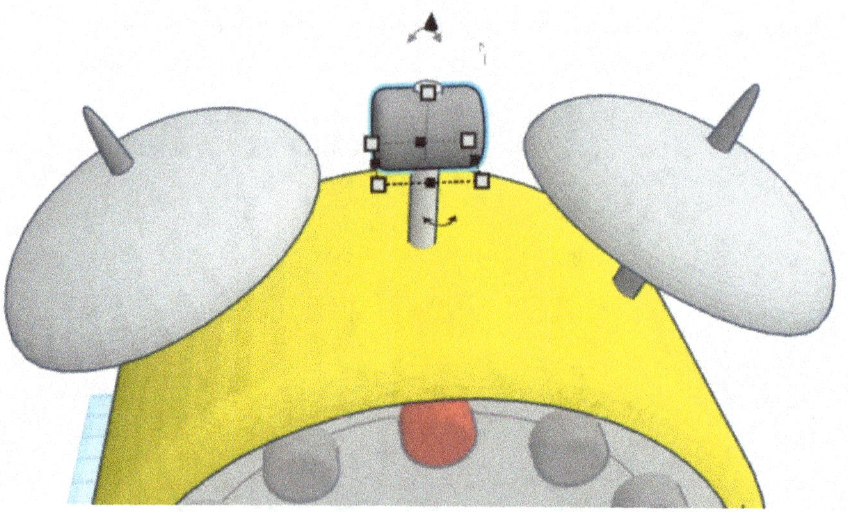

For the on/off switch of the alarm clock, we create two more cylindrical shapes that should have a length and width of about 12 mm and a height of about 20 mm.

One of them we turn by 90 degrees. Then we position the two bodies so that a cross is created. We also change the color, for example to white, and group both bodies.

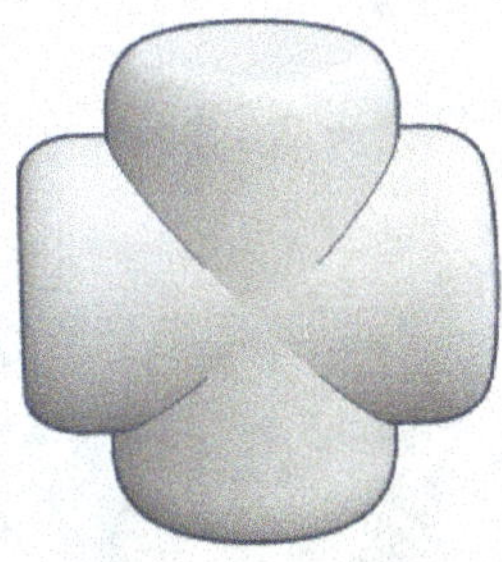

Then we move the switch to the top of the alarm clock and place it in the front area, approximately in the center in front of the hammer.

4.4 The feet and the back of the alarm clock

Now we are almost finished with this project. We just need to create a cover for the back of the alarm clock and two feet. For the back of the alarm clock, we duplicate the yellow case and move it back a bit. If you've already grouped the parts, you'll need to ungroup them for this.

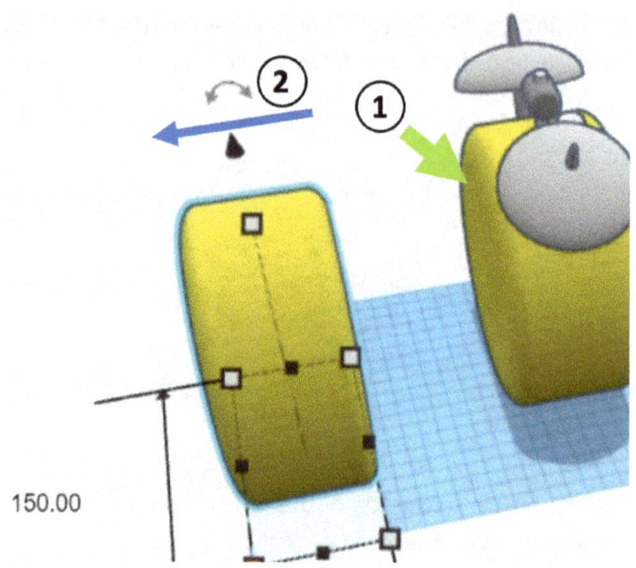

Then we change the dimensions. The thickness of the part should be only 10 mm, the other two dimensions should be 140 mm each.

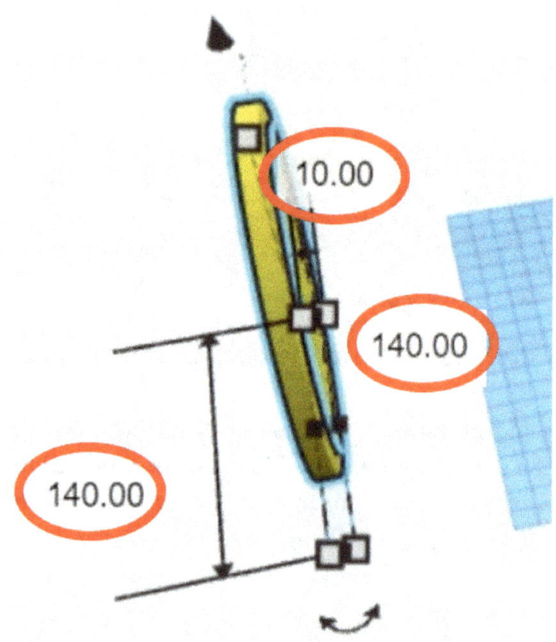

Afterward, we choose a suitable color, e.g., black, and position the lid on the back of the alarm clock using the "Align" command and making shifts with the mouse and keyboard.

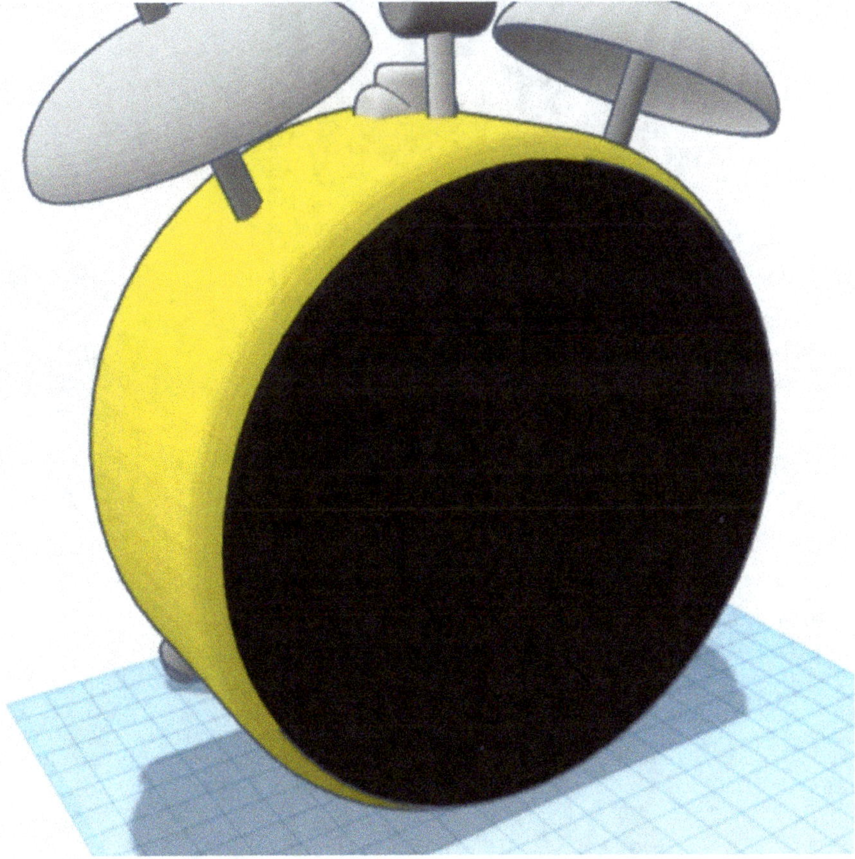

After that, we create the feet of the alarm clock. We put these together from two bodies. We need a cylindrical body ① with 15 mm length and width and approx. 23 mm height and a paraboloid ② with 15 mm length and width and 7 mm height. Furthermore, we assemble the two bodies as shown.

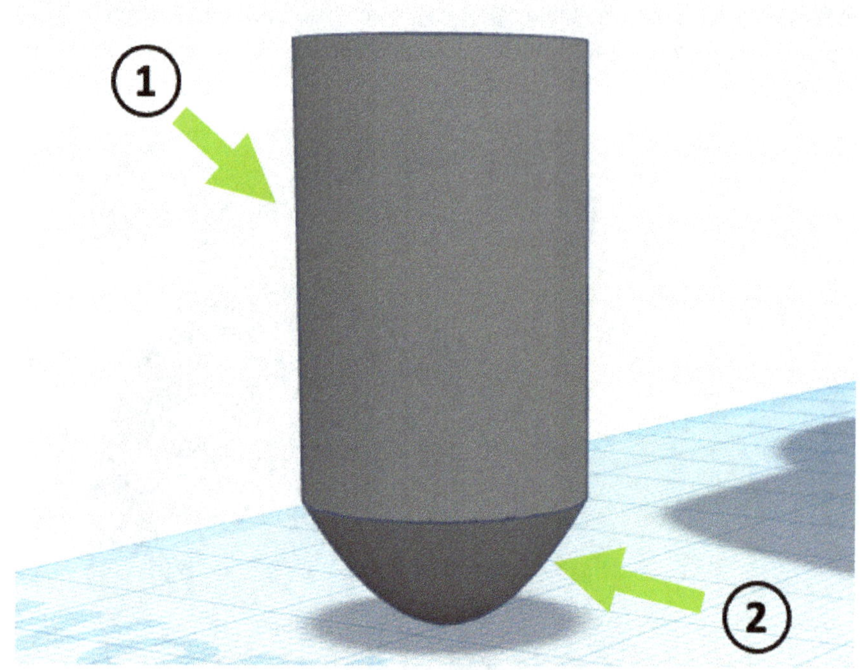

Then two rotations take place. First, we rotate the grouped bodies -22.5 degrees backwards and then 22.5 degrees to the right.

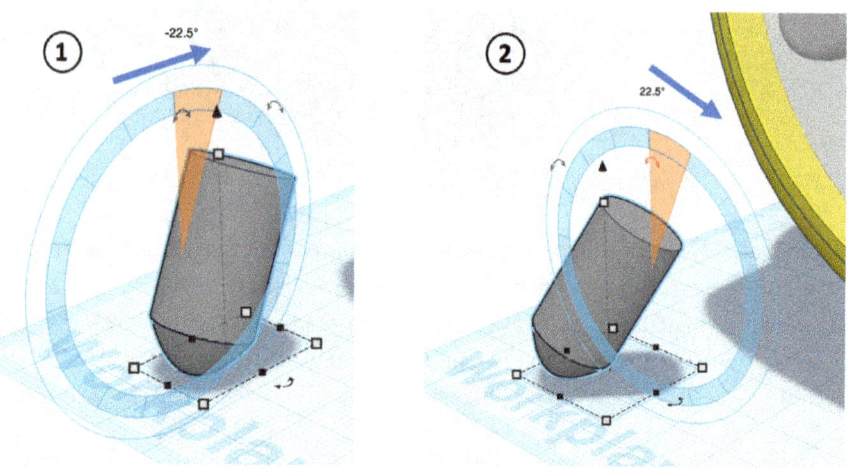

In the next steps we use the two commands "Duplicate and repeat" as well as "Mirror" to create the second foot, which must point in the other direction.

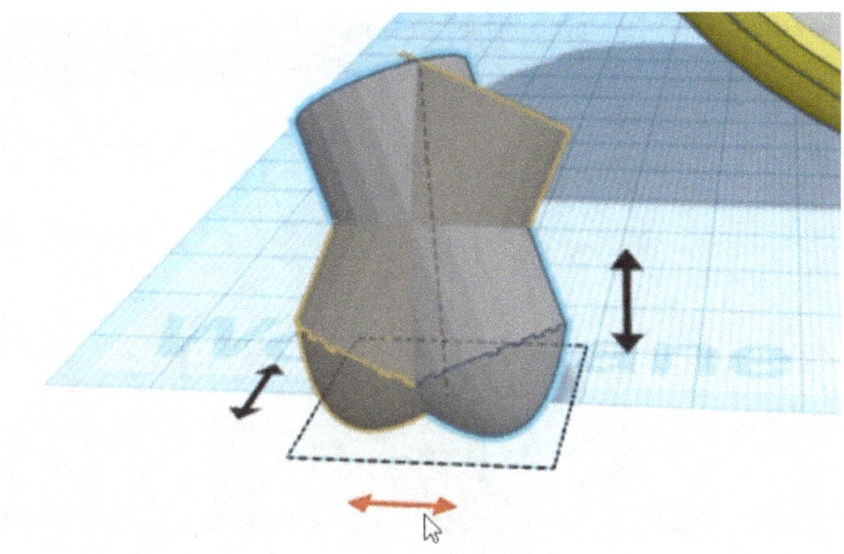

We push the two feet apart a bit and position them in the front area of the alarm clock for now.

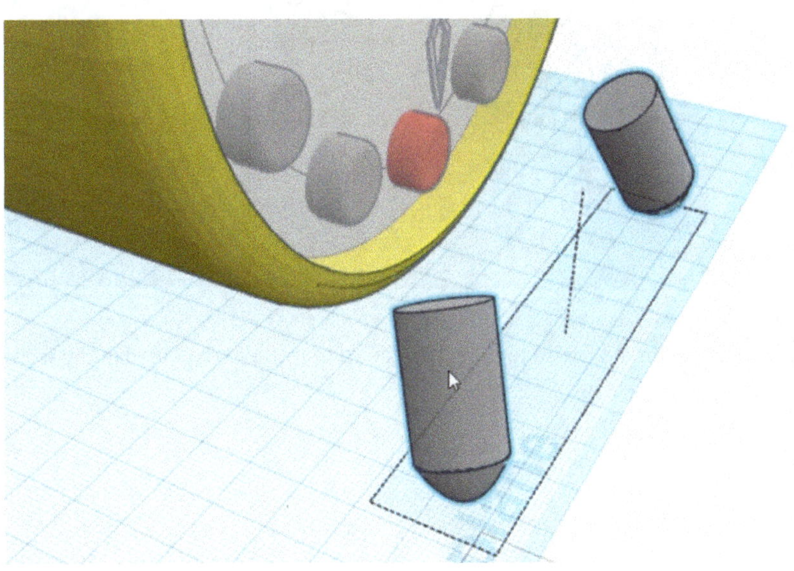

Before we position the feet underneath the alarm clock, we mark all objects of the alarm clock (except the feet) and turn the whole alarm clock backwards by about 12 degrees.

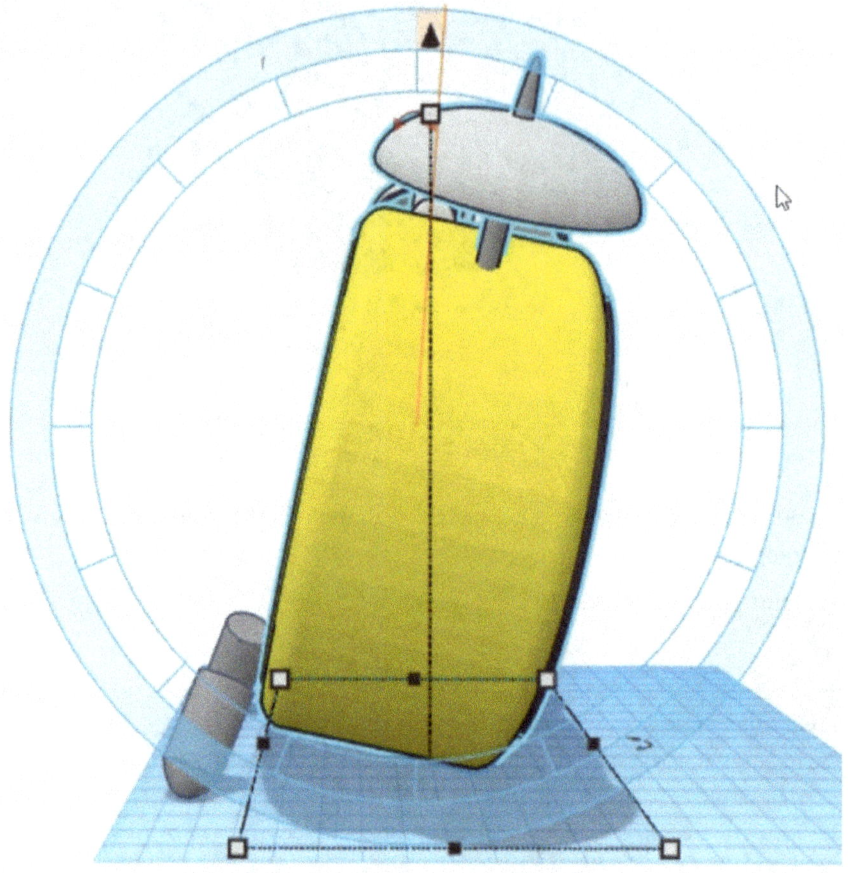

Subsequently, we can move the feet backwards so that they are placed in the front area below the alarm clock.

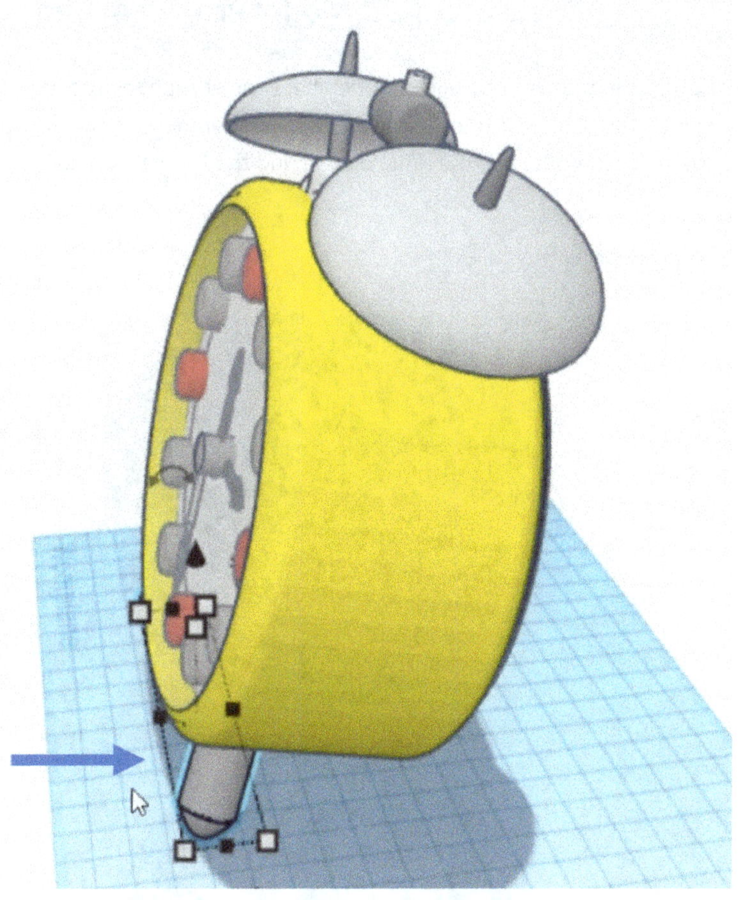

Excellent job! We have successfully finished the chapter. As you may have noticed, the steps in this example were not quite as detailed as in the previous projects. This will help you trust your abilities more and apply what you've learned so far more independently.

However, it is also perfectly okay if you still had difficulties in creating the model. If that's the case, then it's best to work through the chapter or even the whole book a second time from the beginning. If you didn't have any problems, you can now look forward to the next project!

Chapter 5 | 3D Model Project 4: Rim

The project in this chapter will be somewhat shorter than the previous two objects. However, this does not necessarily make it less complex. In this project, we want to create a 3D model of a car rim. You can find the finished model at the following link:

https://tinyurl.com/bdhan49h

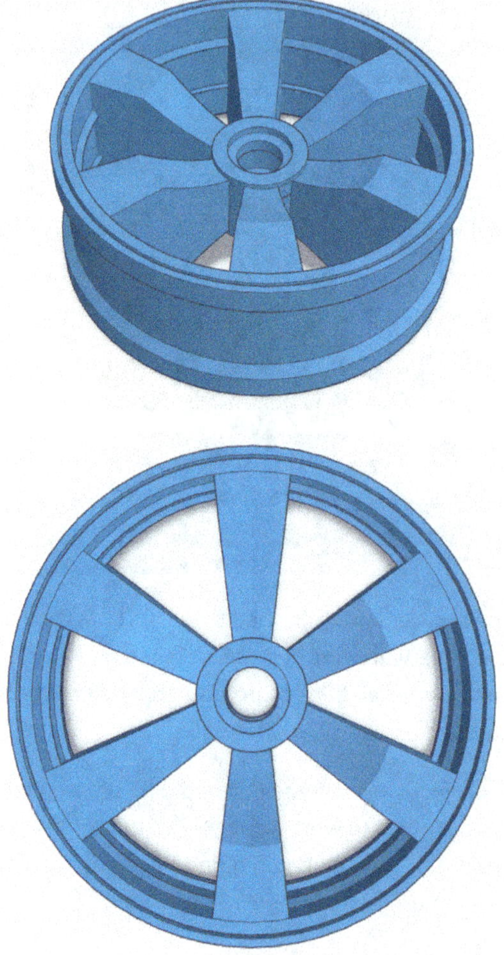

For the rim, we will first start with the construction of the base body. After that, we will create the interior of the rim.

5.1 The basic body of the rim

For the base body, we need a conical shape, the dimensions of which we modify as follows. The dimensions of the base should be 82 mm each and the height 4 mm. We also change the setting "Top Radius " to 9 mm and the setting "Sides" to 64 mm.

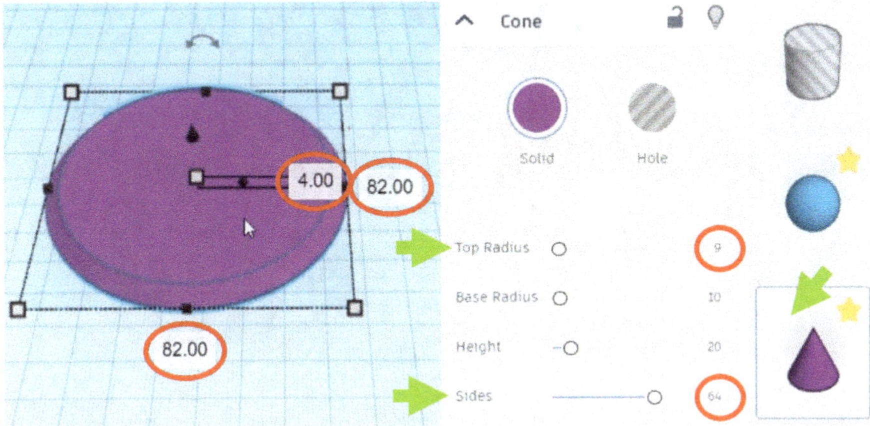

We duplicate this object and change the setting to "Hole". We also change the dimensions of the duplicate (length and width) to 79.5 mm each. We do not change the height and other settings. Thereafter, we move these two bodies to the back for now.

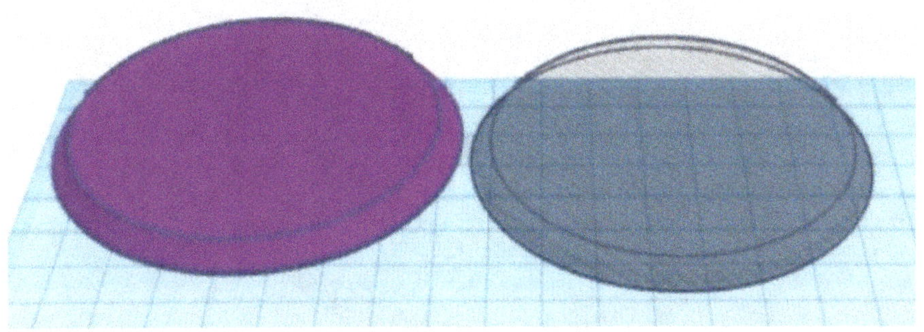

For the second part of the basic body, we need a cylindrical body whose length and width we set to 82 mm each and whose height we set to 5 mm. The parameter "Sides" should again be set to 64 for this body. After we have also duplicated this body, changed its settings to the selection "Hole" and similarly as before, also changed the length and width of the duplicate to 79.5 mm each, we center and group the bodies belonging together. This creates two rings.

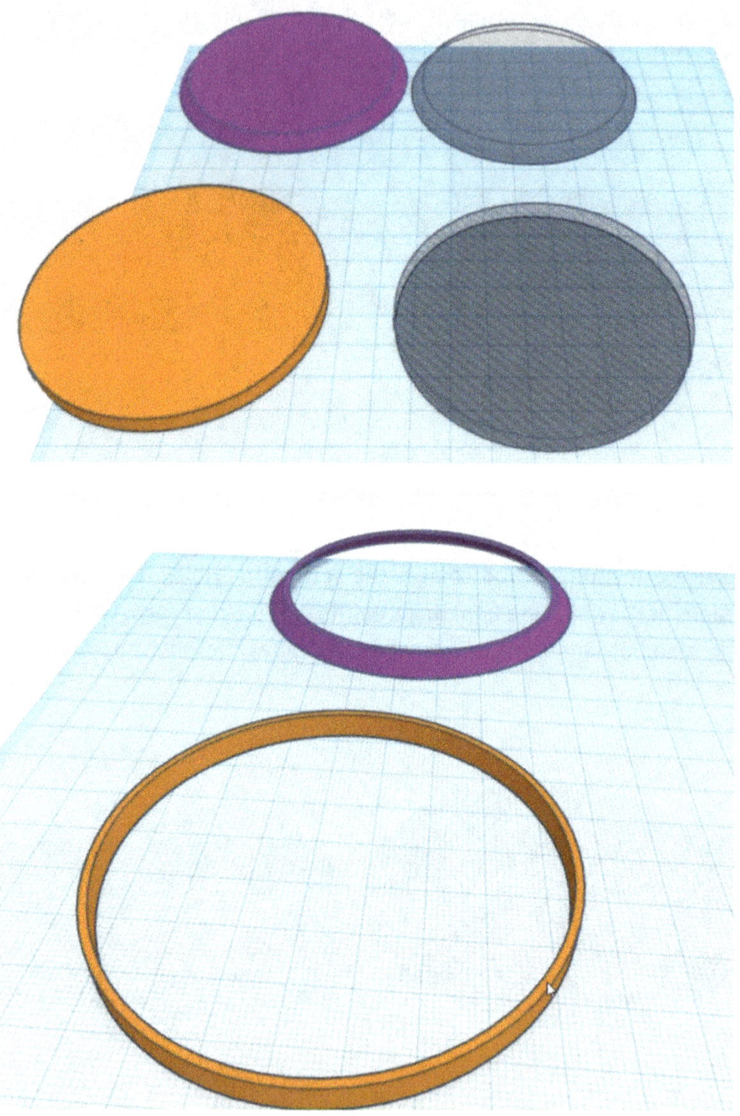

From these two rings, we can now create the first part of the outer base body of the rim. To do this, in the first step we place the conical ring on the cylindrical ring and in the second step we center both using the command "Align". It is also best to use the command Workplane Tool to set the plane on the upper surface of the cylindrical ring and then place the conical ring on this plane using the "D" key.

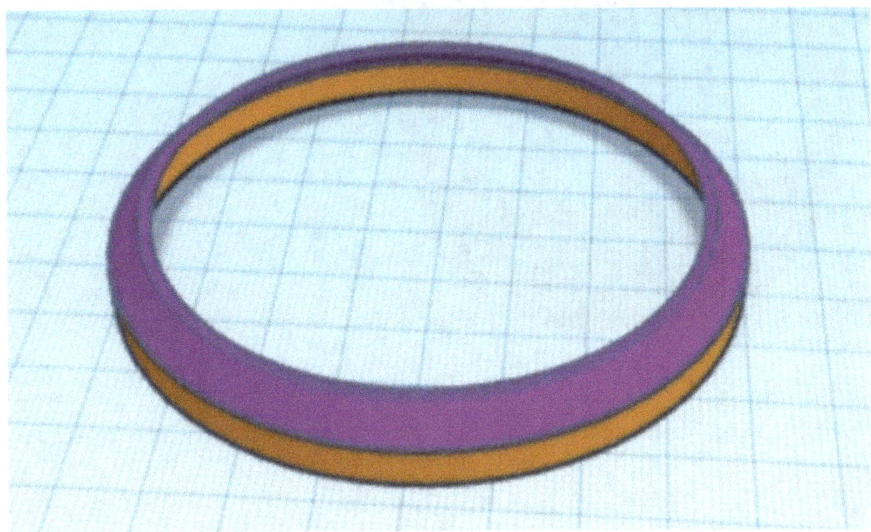

For the central part of the rim, we use the tubular body "Tube", whose dimensions and settings we make as shown.

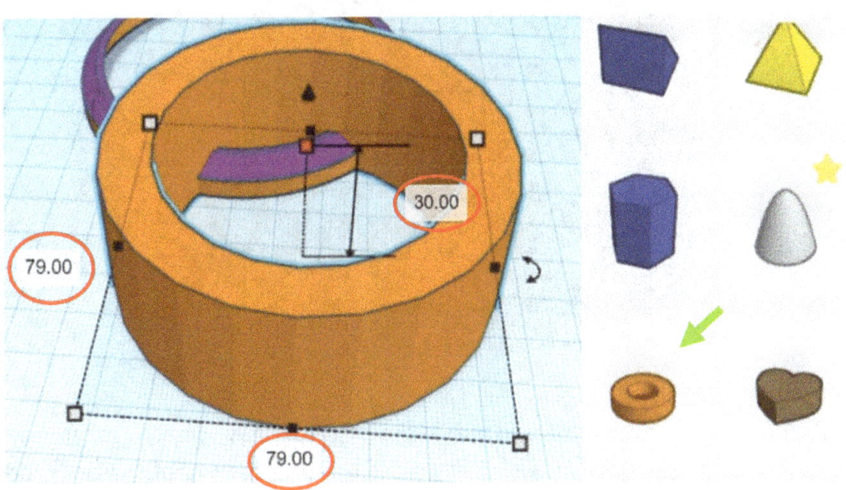

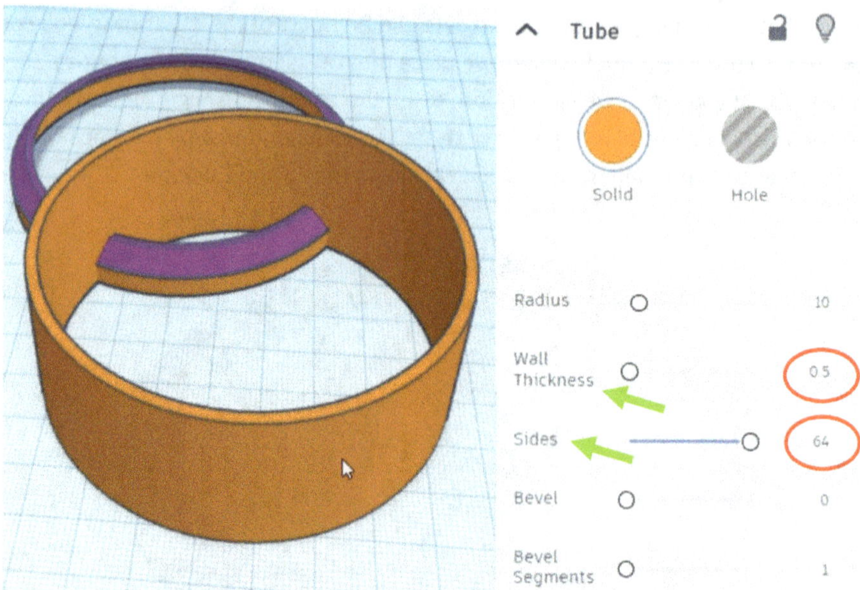

Using the "Align" command, we can then center all the bodies we have created so far.

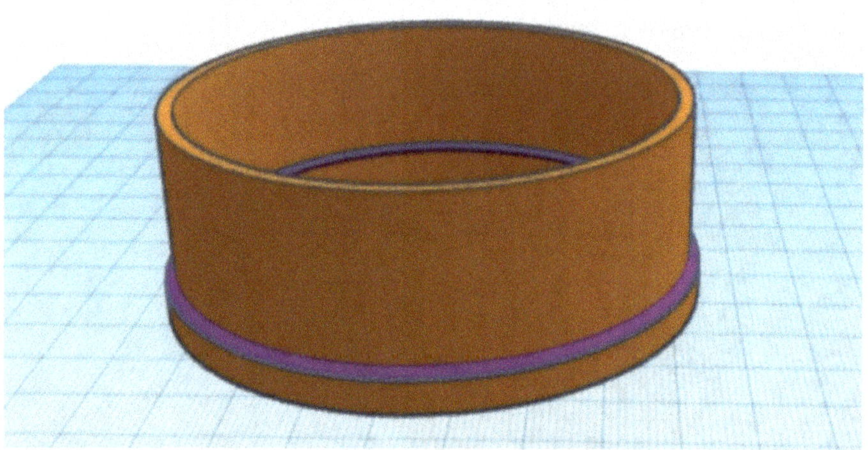

In the next step, we duplicate and mirror the object we have created so far, using the shortcuts "CTRL+D" and "M". Our goal is to make the top of the body look exactly opposite to the bottom. We achieve this by selecting the displayed double-arrow (the vertical one) when flipping.

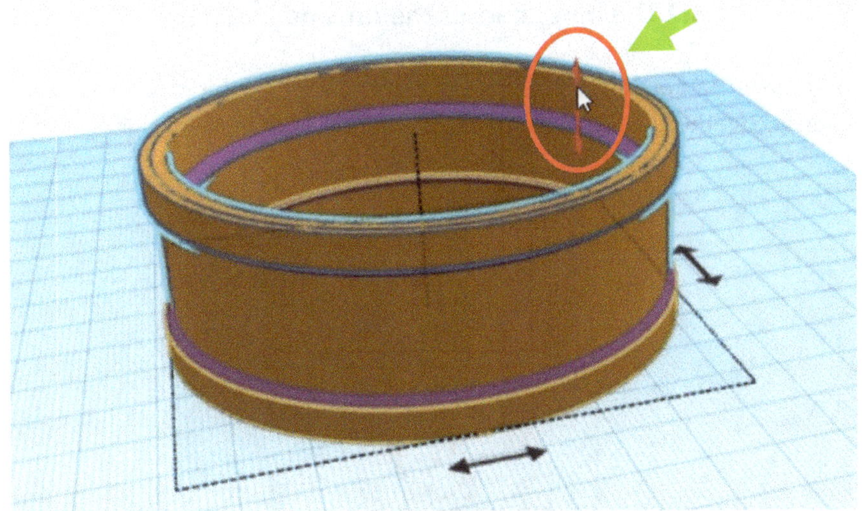

After that, we can change the color of the object created so far as shown. And since mistakes also happen to me, I reduce the basic dimensions of the tubular central body (white) by 1 mm to the actually required 78 mm in the next step.

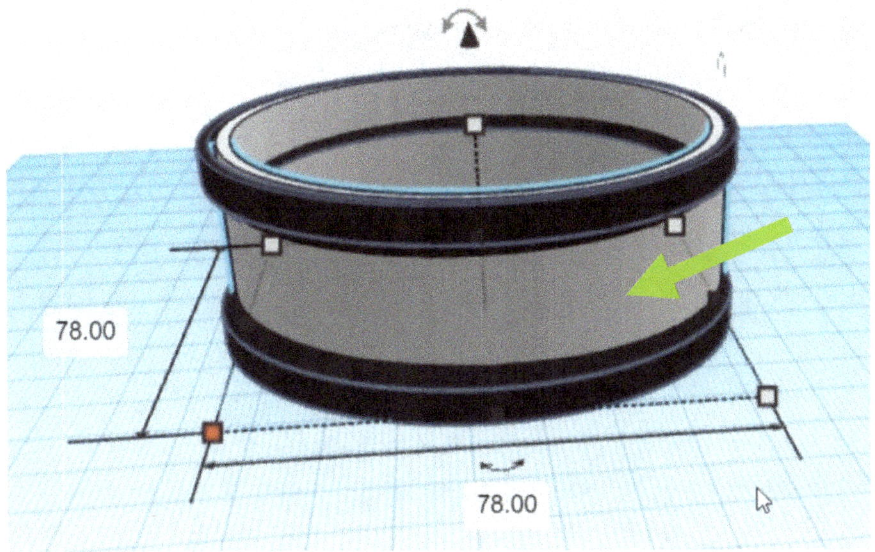

Subsequently, I had to center the objects again, and did move them to the side or back for now.

5.2 The inner part of the rim and assembly

For the inner part of the rim, we first create the struts, the basis of which is a cube-shaped body. This should be 32 mm long, 14 mm wide and 15 mm high.

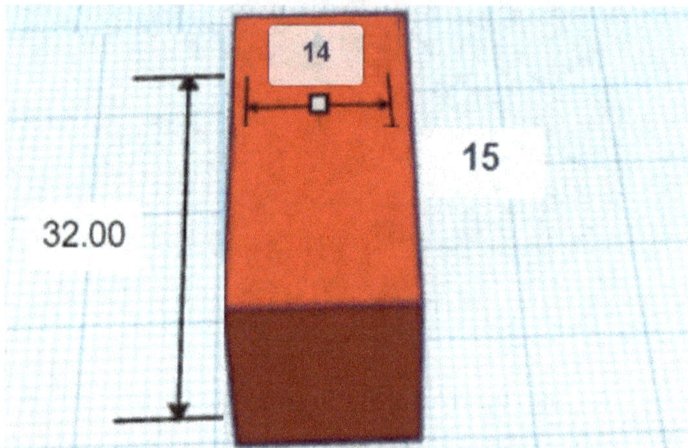

Then we cut away two parts of the side faces from this body to change the shape. We do this with a cube-shaped body with the "Hole" setting, which we first drag to 60 mm in length and then rotate by -6 degrees.

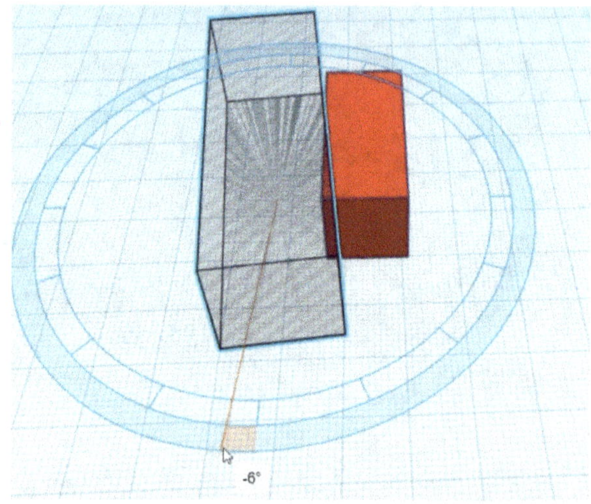

We then duplicate and mirror the body so that we can also change the shape of the opposite side. The alignment of the two bodies should then be done approximately as shown. This is done using the command "Align" and selecting the two center alignment points.

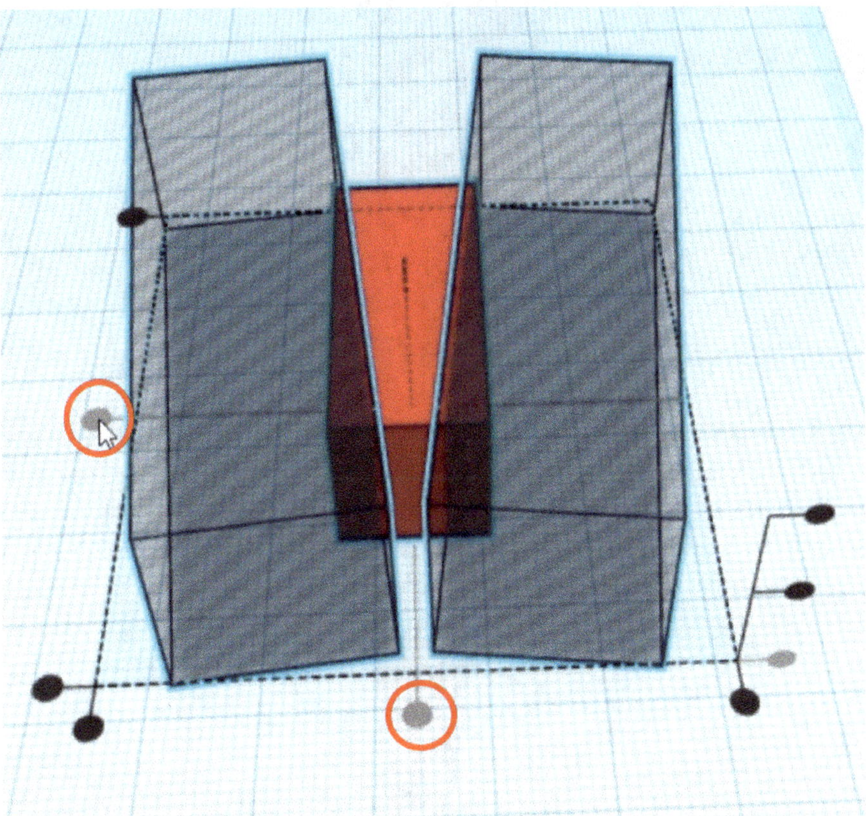

Since the spacing between the transparent bodies is not apparent in this arrangement, and therefore may be a bit difficult for some to recreate, here is a link that contains the finished brace:

https://tinyurl.com/bde7ppea

So if you didn't manage the arrangement well, you can check here again by splitting the strut with "Ungroup", or just copy the whole object with "CTRL+C" and paste it into your project with "CTRL+V".

After grouping, the strut should look like this.

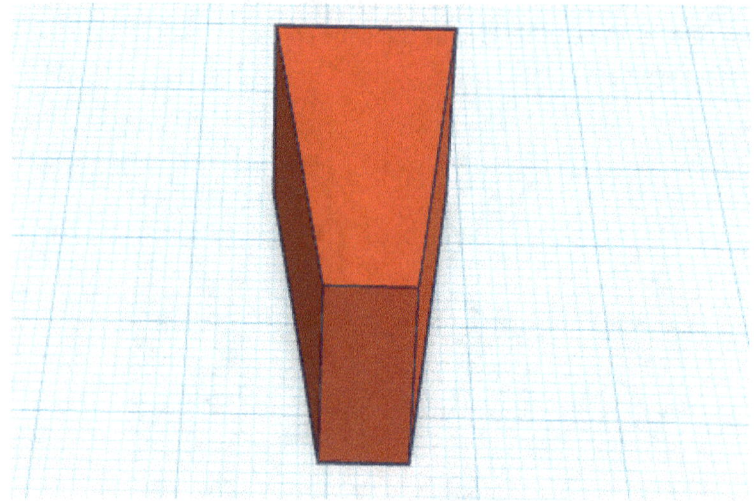

We now need a lot of these struts, which we arrange in a circle around a tubular object. Therefore, in the next step, we get the tubular body "Tube" onto our work plane. Furthermore, we need a cube (setting: "Hole"), which we will use as a placeholder between two opposite struts. We shorten the length of the cube to 14 mm, leaving the other dimensions at the preset values.

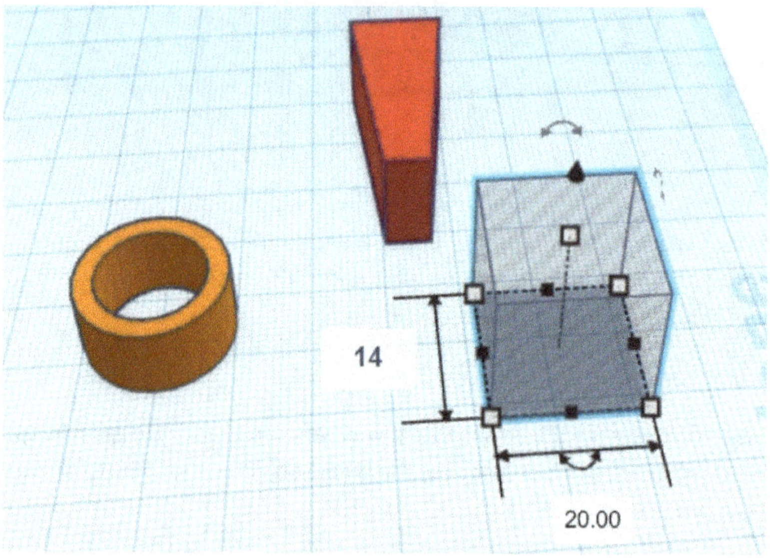

The second opposite strut, which I mentioned earlier, you can get quite simply by duplicating and mirroring. The further arrangement succeeds with the command "Workplane Tool" and by pressing the "D" key. The centering you can make, of course, with the command "Align".

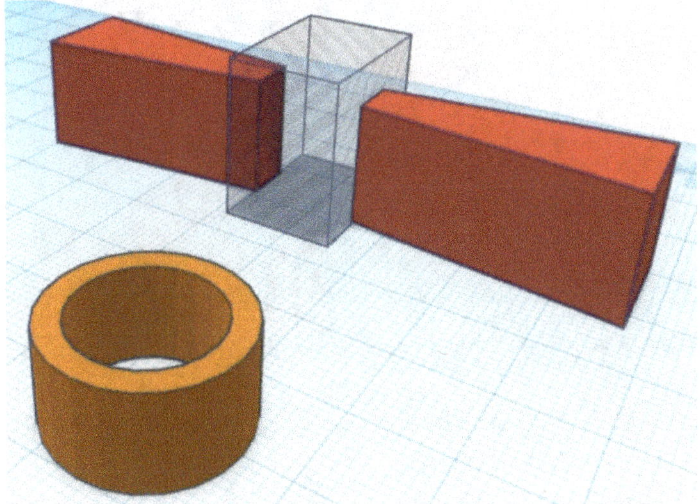

Then we can delete the cube-shaped body, which only served as a placeholder. Now we make a few changes to the tubular body. We change the height to 7.5 mm, the wall thickness to 5 mm and the value for "Sides" to 64.

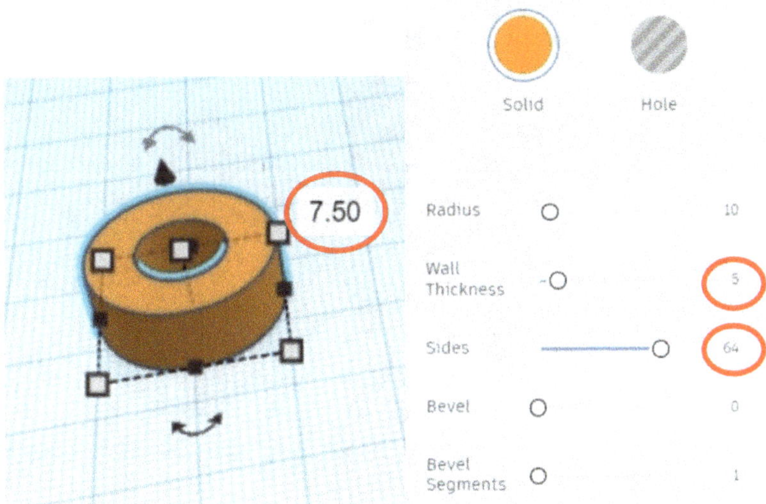

Then we group the two red struts, duplicate them and rotate the duplicate 60 degrees counterclockwise.

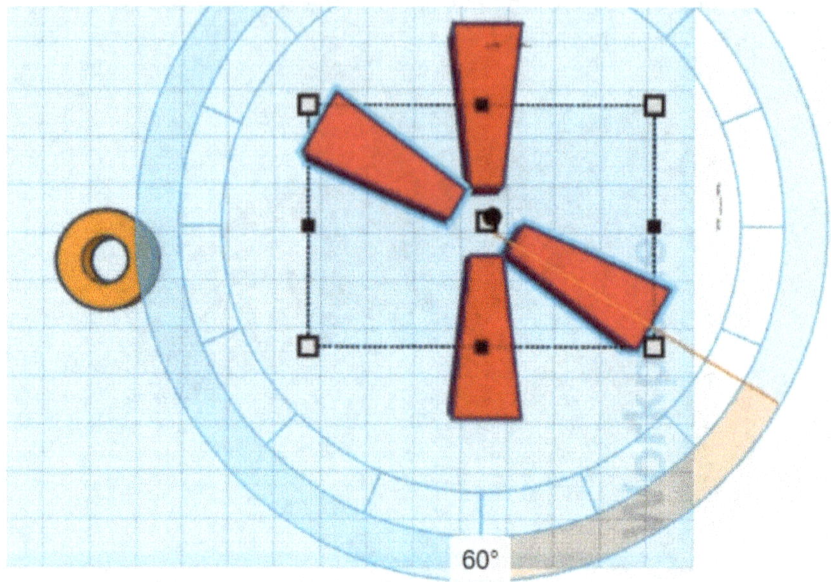

We then duplicate the rotated struts once again. These are also placed with a 60-degree rotation, creating the following star-shaped construct, which we also group ("CTRL+G").

Furthermore, we duplicate the tubular object and place the duplicate in the center area ① of the star-shaped construct. This can be done with the shortcut "L" and by selecting the middle alignment points ②-④.

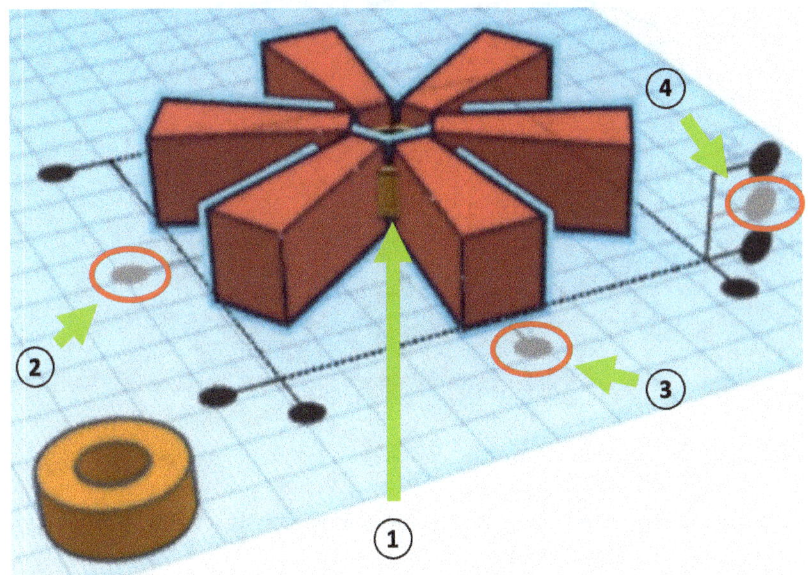

For further refinement of the geometry we need a paraboloid, whose length and width we change to 60 mm each and whose height we change to 12 mm. We want to create a cutout with this body, so we change the settings from "Solid" to "Hole".

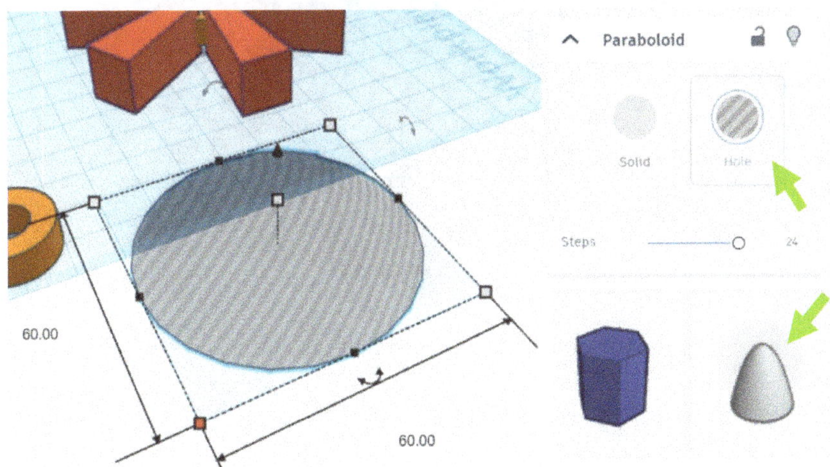

Then we mirror the body with the short command "M" so that the convex curvature points downwards.

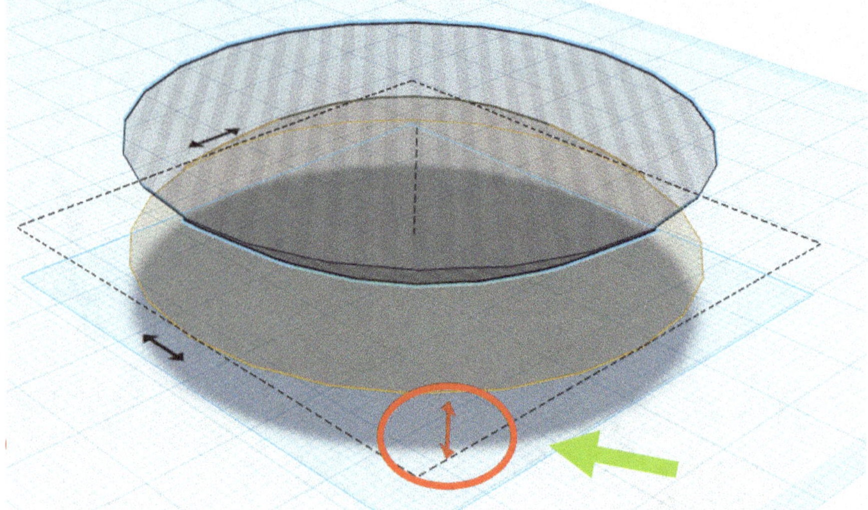

We also center the object within the star-shaped construct and move it up until the distance to the ground is 6 mm.

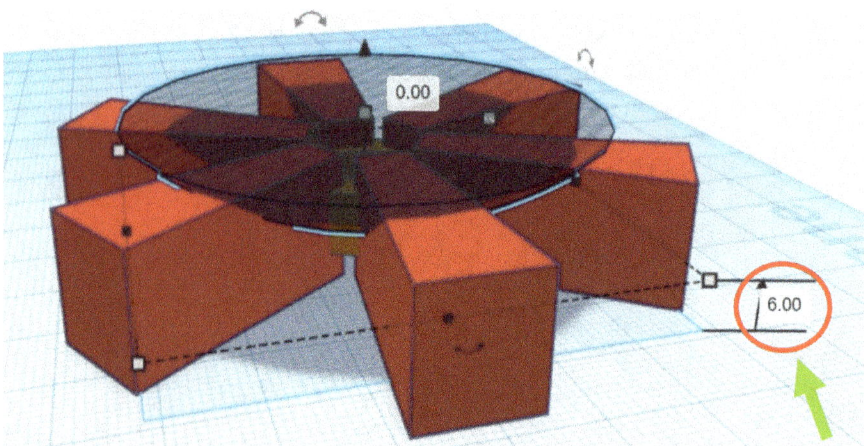

After that, we group the objects together so that the cutting process is performed.

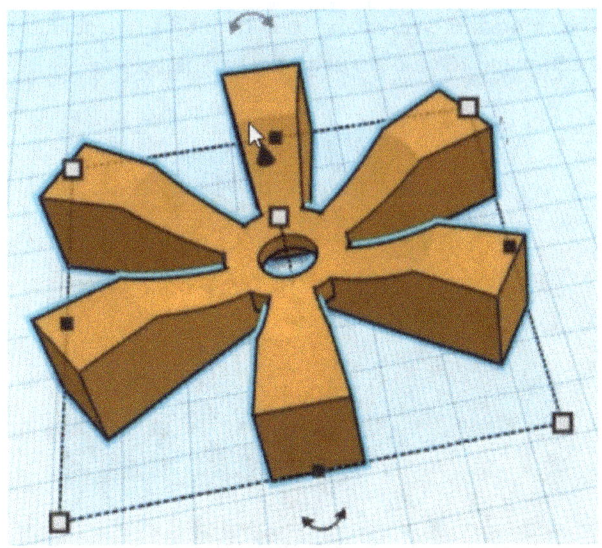

In the next step, we duplicate ("CTRL+D") the grouped object ① and move the duplicate ② slightly upwards. We mirror the initial object in the lower area with the short command "L" and the alignment arrow ③ as shown. The two objects should then be aligned exactly opposite to each other.

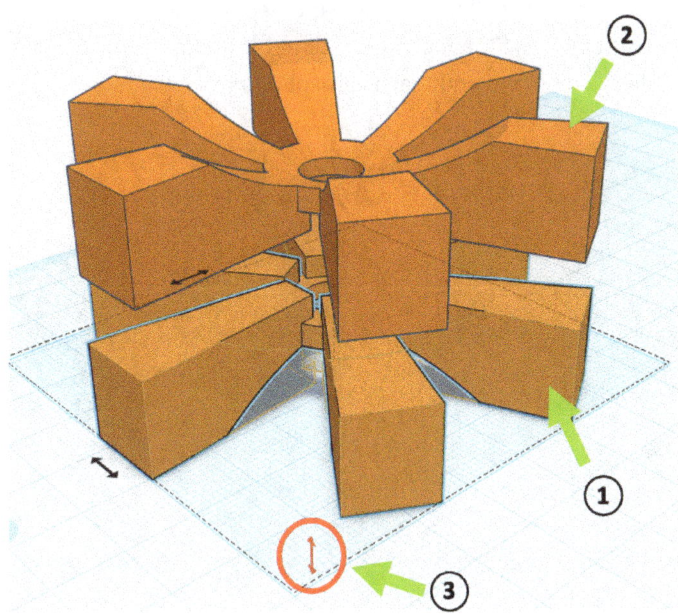

Then we use the command "Workplane Tool" to put the two objects on top of each other and the command "Group" to unite the two objects.

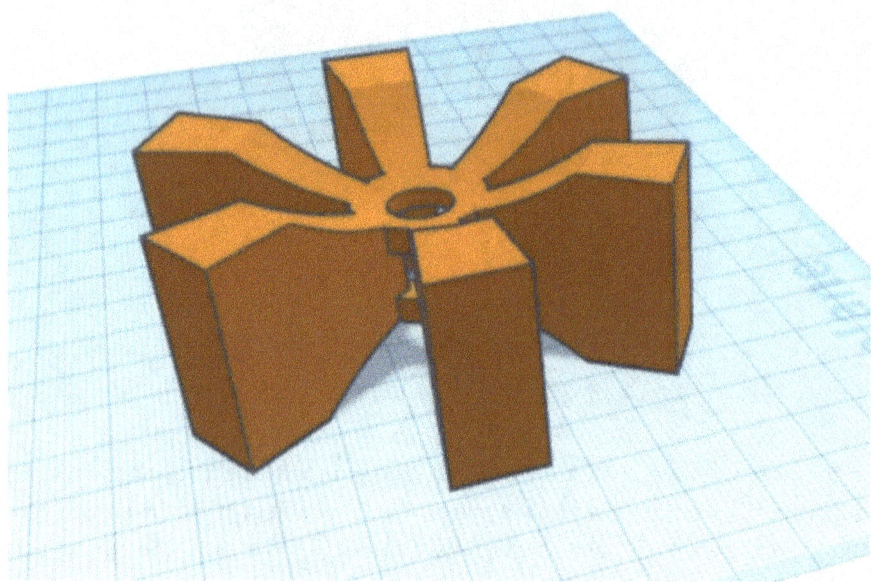

From an earlier step, we still have a tubular object ①, which we use in this step. We change its height to 17 mm and then center it in the middle ② of our object using the "Align" command and the alignment points shown.

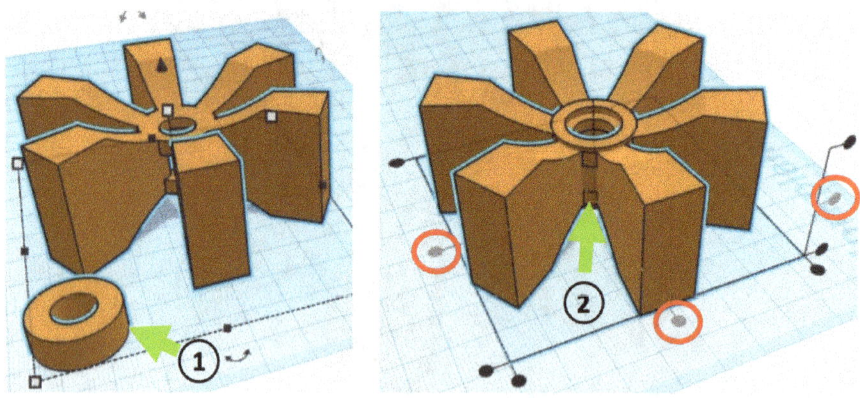

Now the inner part of the rim is done. In the last step we group both the outer part and the inner part and then move them into each other. Using the command "Align", we center the two grouped part objects.

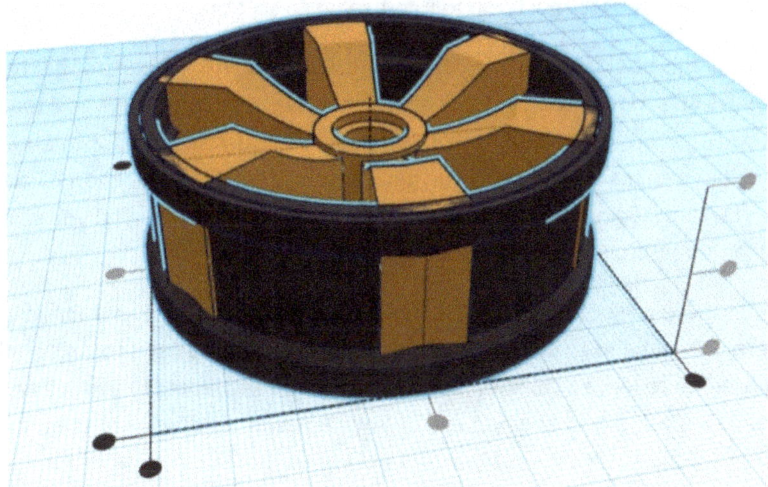

Finally, we change the color and reduce the inner part to 28.75 mm by dragging the marked point so that the struts no longer pierce the outer part of the rim.

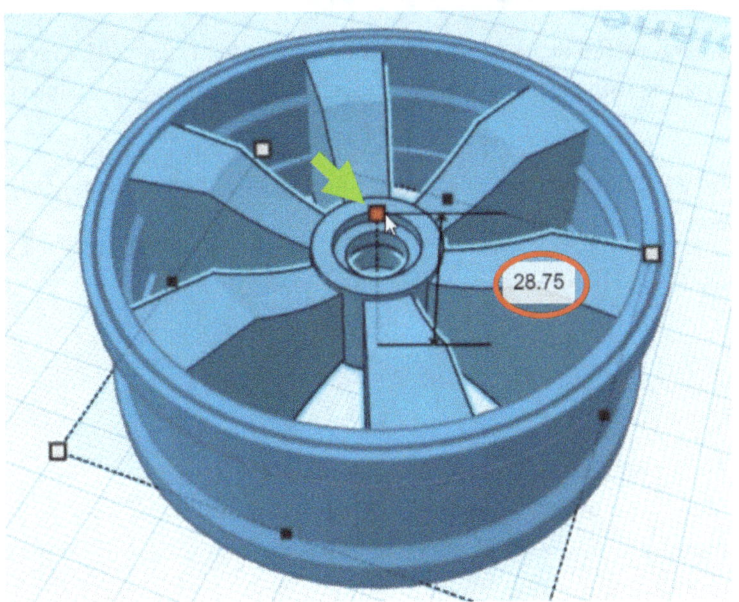

Closing words

Bravo! You made it to the end of the course, that's really impressive! There were some complex steps to master in this course.

The goal of this book was to strengthen your CAD skills with "Tinkercad" by creating impressive 3D models step by step. I hope that we have achieved this goal together and you got some great benefit from this book. We have created a total of four remarkable designs and thereby further consolidated the application of already known features. So, you have every reason to be proud of yourself if you've made it this far. Congratulations!

Whether there will be another sequel for this second part with even more creative CAD projects remains to be seen and also depends on the reviews for this book. So don't hesitate to leave a review if you liked the book and would like to see another sequel to it. Please also keep an eye on my "Amazon" author page to stay up to date.

You are welcome to check out my other books on topics like 3D printing, and more advanced CAD programs like "Fusion 360" or "FreeCAD" or also on electronics and programming with "Tinkercad" and get a copy if you are interested.

If you are interested in even more in-depth work with "Tinkercad", I recommend you get started with my book "Arduino Projects with Tinkercad" if you haven't tried it yet.

Just have a look at the following pages, there you will find a thematically sorted overview of all my books.

Thanks again and hope to see you next time!

Books on topics you might also like

All books are available online on the usual sales platforms. It's best to just search for the title, or feel free to visit my author page. Some of the books may not be published yet and will be released or found soon. Take a look at the books of your choice and your copy as e-book or paperback!

3D Printing:

CAD, FEM, CAM (3D Object Creation, Design, Simulation):

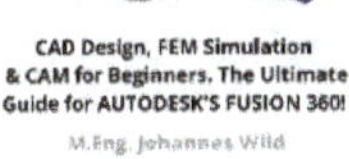
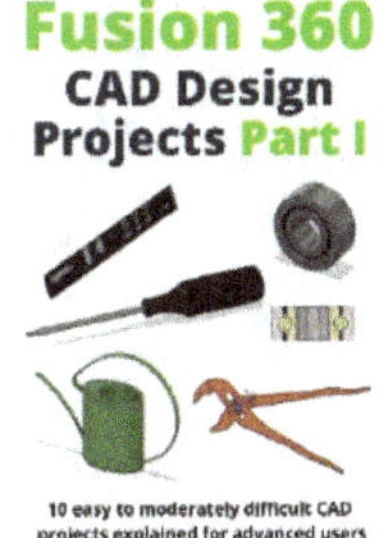
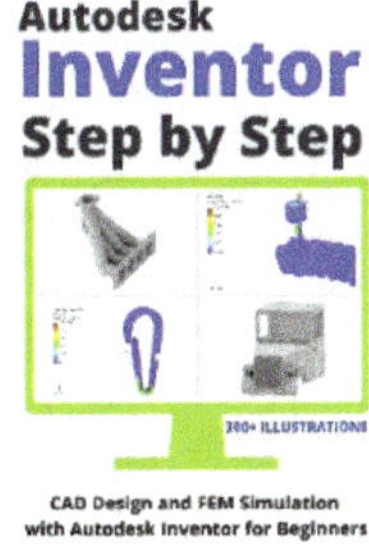

Electrical Engineering:

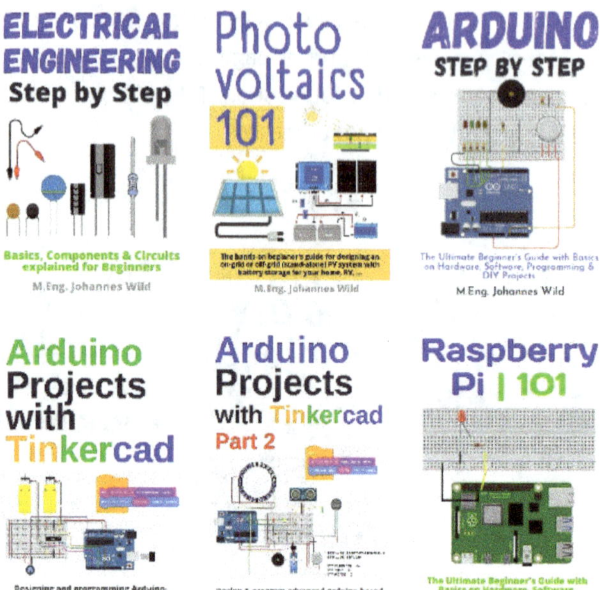

Programming and other Software:

There are also identical video courses for some of these books:

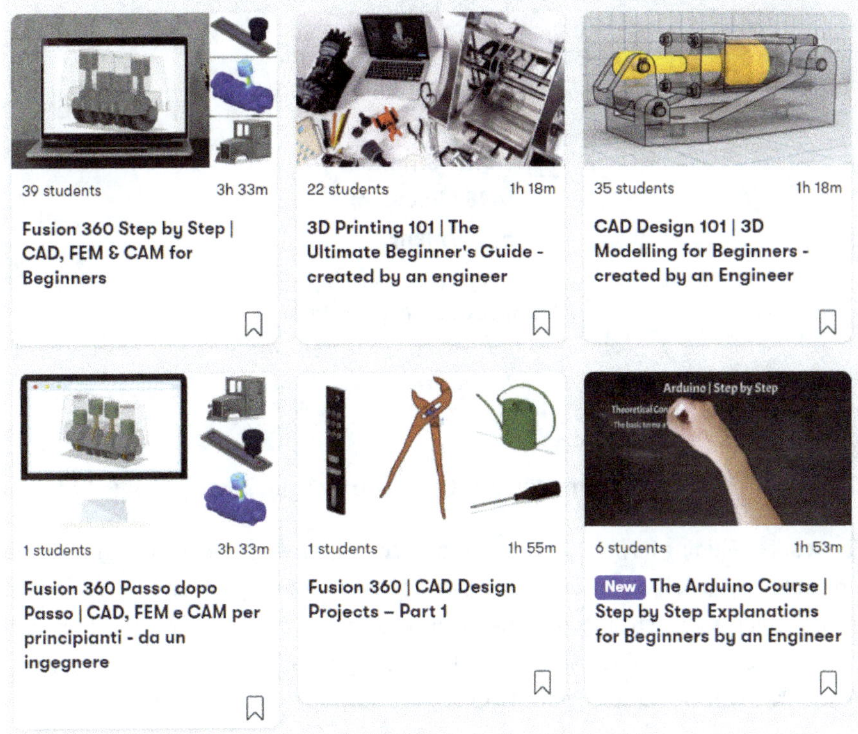

They are hosted on the learning website: skillshare.com

Be sure to use my following friends & family referral link to get a month of membership for free!

(I will get a little bonus if you choose to stay, so we will be both happy. Thanks in advance!)

https://www.skillshare.com/r/profile/Johannes-Wild/854541251

It is best to copy the link in your browser to access the free month!

Sign up today and deepen your knowledge!

Imprint of the author / publisher

© 2024

Johannes Wild
c/o RA Matutis
Berliner Straße 57
14467 Potsdam
Germany

Email: 3dtech@gmx.de

This work is protected by copyright

Thank you so much for choosing this book!

9 783987 421228